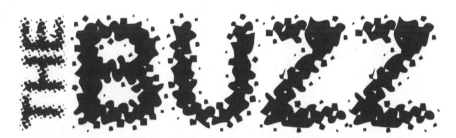

THE BUZZ

A practical confidence builder for teenagers

David Hodgson

Crown House Publishing Limited
www.crownhouse.co.uk

First published by

Crown House Publishing Ltd
Crown Buildings, Bancyfelin, Carmarthen, Wales, SA33 5ND, UK
www.crownhouse.co.uk

and

Crown House Publishing Company LLC
6 Trowbridge Drive, Suite 5, Bethel, CT 06801-2858, USA
www.CHPUS.com

British Library of Cataloguing-in-Publication Data
A catalogue entry for this book is available
from the British Library.

10-digit ISBN 190442481-3
13-digit ISBN 978-190442481-9

LCCN 2006929710

Designed and typeset by Thomas Fitton

Printed and bound in the UK by
Cromwell Press
Trowbridge
Wiltshire

Acknowledgements

The Buzz pulls together all of the most useful theory, research and practice I've encountered over the past twenty years in which I've worked with people to help them make better decisions and achieve their best. I'm particularly indebted to those who have developed Personality Type Theory and NLP I find that both approaches can really help people discover and realize their true potential. I hope *The Buzz* encourages people to look further into these approaches.

I'd also like to thank all of the people I've worked with, clients and colleagues, who have helped me develop the theory into a practical and useful format.

Thank you to everyone at Crown House Publishing for helping unleash *The Buzz* to a wider audience.

For Cathy, Daniel and Lucy.

CONTENTS

Section One – Make Your Personality Buzz   1

i

Section Two – Make Your Behaviour Buzz 75

Part Three – Go For It   123

Appendix

Introduction

John is an experienced skydiver. Eighteen months ago he jumped out of a plane. It was a beautiful sunny day.

He pulled the cord to release his parachute and it didn't work. 'Not to worry,' he thought, 'I'll pull the cord for my spare'. It didn't work. It is very rare for both parachutes to fail. The result is usually death, painful but quick. John thought he had about thirty seconds left of life. His final thought would be, 'I wish I'd done more with my life.' This is common.

Luckily, John landed in soft snow and survived. This is rare. He spent a year in hospital recovering from his injuries. He then saw me, a careers adviser, because he wanted to make something of himself, to use his potential, not waste his life. John said that as he fell, certain he would die, he marked his life on a scale of 0 to 10. He was disappointed because he gave himself a 6. He wished he'd done more with the skills and strengths he has.

If you were to mark your life out of 10, what score would you give yourself?

A 10 means you've fully used all the potential, opportunities and skills you have. Zero means you've completely wasted your life so far. John was one of the first to use *The Buzz* to help him achieve his best. Since John, thousands of others have joined him.

- **10:** I've fully lived my life to my true potential.
- **8–9:** I've mostly made the most of my skills and strengths.
- **6–7:** I'm doing OK, but …
- **3–5:** I've probably wasted a lot of the opportunities I've had.
- **0–2:** Oh, dear!

John gives two bits of advice to people – use *The Buzz,* and check your parachutes carefully before you jump.

What score would you like?

Like John, use *The Buzz* to take your score as high as you dare!

Kelly Holmes, Darth Vader and Shrek

The Buzz will help you be your best – it's easier than you think. I asked about a hundred teenagers, 'What do you want from your life?'

They all said, basically, the same three things: to be happy, confident and feel I did my best. With *The Buzz* you can have all three.

Most life stories follow the same pattern.

In Shrek, the hero finds out who he is: an ogre with a heart forced to live alone because others judge him by how he looks. He then finds out what he wants from life – Fiona – and finally he goes for it. These three steps are the same for Luke and Darth Vader in *Star Wars*, David and Victoria Beckham, Kelly Holmes and all of us.

- Step One: Finding out who we are.
- Step Two: Finding out what makes us buzz.
- Step Three: Deciding to go for it.

The Buzz is in three sections to help you address these areas in your life:

Section One: Make Your Personality Buzz

Discover   your personality preferences;

what you're naturally good at – with career ideas;

how to get on better with friends and family.

Section Two: Make Your Behaviour Buzz

Discover   how we 'do' moods;

positive and negative directions, mood control;

the best of all ten personality strengths.

Section Three: Go For It

Discover   seven ways to really buzz;
more confidence and less stress;
how to be your best.

Great inventors and farts

Our brain is an amazing thing. It is the most complicated known thing in the universe.

Sometimes it helps make us believe we can do amazing things – great inventions, acts of incredible bravery – when we are at our best. Then sometimes we do daft things such as touching wet paint to check it's wet because we can't believe the sign, or lighting farts. Two people die each year from lighting their own farts. What a sad (and painful!) way to die. Sometimes we move in a negative direction and are not our best!

It is better to understand how our brain works and control it for the life we really want, rather than stick to habits that hinder us. Most people use about 10 per cent of their potential.

With *The Buzz*, you can access the other 90 per cent. How much of it do you dare use?

Question: Are there more neuron cells in your brain or people on earth?
Answer: at the bottom of Page ix.

Mind magic

Some scientists once proved that bumblebees couldn't fly. Their wings just weren't strong enough to lift their bodies. Nobody told the bumblebees! The bee's brain believes it can fly, so it flaps its wings until it does, and they can fly at over 48 kilometres (30 miles) per hour. We are the same: we have more potential than we realise. We can use our own brains to believe things that move us in a positive direction and remove beliefs that take us in a negative direction.

Our brains make many assumptions for us. Can you see the white triangle? Most people can, even though it isn't there.

Brain power

Our brain receives more than 2 million pieces of information every second, so it simplifies things for us all of the time. Our brains make us believe things: some good, some bad, some useful and some useless. Once we recognise this, we can control our brains to become happier and more confident, and be our best.

The Buzz has been developed with and used by thousands of young people. It works. Try it. Enjoy it. Let it help you be your best. Millions of adults wait until they're old before they go for it (some never do).

Remember the tingle of excitement we get as young children on Christmas morning, or birthdays, seeing the presents in front of us, wondering what is there, knowing there will be some surprises? This buzz is something people have all the time when they are happy, confident and at their best.

Start now

The best comments I receive from young people using *The Buzz* are about their surprise at how easy it can be to start living a great life, discovering new strengths and skills, dreaming dreams, planning to make them happen and enjoying feeling great while moving in a positive direction that feels right.

We can build a great life around our strengths, the things we enjoy and are good at.

The Buzz also shows us simple ways in which we can alter our behaviour to succeed in the different situations and challenges we face.

Enjoy finding out about yourself and others.

 ## Warning!

- The learning is in the doing.
- We remember 90 per cent of what we say and do.
- We remember only 10 per cent of what we read.

So don't just read *The Buzz*: do it! There are games to play throughout *The Buzz*. They are clearly marked.

For best results, read through the whole book – *slowly*. Take your time, like a group of twelve-year-olds at McDonald's who can make a small milkshake last for three hours on a Saturday afternoon. Slurp on!

If at any time you get bored, just add your favourite rude words to some of the sentences. This technique has helped my children through many a dull reading book from arse school. Did you spot that one?

Answer to question on Page vii: There are far more neuron cells in your brain (more than 100 billion) than people on Earth (6.5 billion).

Section One

Make Your Personality Buzz

Make Your Personality Buzz

What kind of personality do you have?

In this section, we'll explore type theory to help uncover some of your natural strengths.

Be a superhero

If you could be a superhero, what would your special power be?

Invisible? Amazingly strong?

Think of what you're good at now and exaggerate these qualities.

When I was young, I was cute and quiet. So perhaps my superhero qualities would be Mr Shh (so quiet that he could be invisible) or Mr Ah (so cute that evil villains would trust him, allowing him to foil their dastardly plans).

So who could you be?

Most people struggle to say what they're good at because they are either too modest or they really don't know.

Can you choose three positive words that sum up your personality?

_____   _____   _____

Which of the words under 'Personality buzzwords' on Page 4 best describe you? Will they match those in your personality profile?

Personality direction

Which way are you facing?

Many studies have revealed five big chunks of personality. For each of these, we can face one way or the other. We can breathe in or breathe out. Both part of the same thing but opposite directions. In personality, we can point each way: sometimes we're quiet; at other times we may be very chatty. But mostly we face one way – our preference. When we have a choice of doing something two ways, we always seem to pick one and stick with it. This is why, when we put our pants on in the morning, we always put the same leg in first! Adding up our preferences can reveal a lot about our personality and behaviour. We can also explore ways to develop and use the best of all ten. Most people use five out of the ten. With *The Buzz,* you can go for ten out of ten.

Ask a friend if they agree. What will they like best about you?

Next, look at the five chunks of personality from Pages 12 to 28.

Remember, there are no right or wrong answers. Just choose your preference.

Personality buzzwords

Tick the words that match your personality. Ask a friend if they agree. What will they like best about you?

Achiever

Someone who gets things done even when things get tough.

Analytical

Works things out carefully, paying attention to detail and facts.

Caring

Will look after other people or animals.

Determined

Stick up for themselves, their friends and their beliefs until things are sorted out.

Enthusiastic

Get excited about things and get other people excited too.

Flexible

Willing to try new things and not scared to learn from experience.

Friendly

Make other people feel good and relaxed.

Funny

A good sense of humour, fun to be with.

Generous

Share their time, money and thoughts without expecting something in return.

Imaginative

Come up with good ideas and new ways to do things.

Independent

Make decisions on their own, don't just follow the crowd.

Organised

Plan their time carefully so they can get more done and worry less.

Loyal

Stay friends through good times and bad.

Modest

Doesn't show off or brag about their successes.

Practical

Get things done, don't just talk about it.

Reliable

Do what they say they will; someone you can trust.

 Tip:

These can be great words to use in your CV.

Can you guess which one of these famous people has the same personality as you?

Victoria Beckham

When she was younger, she is said to have stated that her ambition was to become a brand as famous as Nike or Daz. She has certainly achieved this goal by using her knowledge of how the media and business work to full effect. She is determined, confident and hardworking to make the most of her talents. An achiever who gets things done. Do you share these qualities?

David Beckham

Famous footballer and former England captain who is naturally talented but is also prepared to practise long hours to be the best footballer he can be. Quiet, friendly, down-to-earth, organised, determined, reliable, caring and hardworking. Do you share these qualities?

Bridget Jones

Famous from the film/novel *Bridget Jones's Diary*. Usually says what she's thinking; resulting in embarrassment. She gets away with it because she is fun-loving, enthusiastic, generous and caring. A bit disorganised, but her heart is in the right place. Do you share these qualities?

Michael Palin

Famous comedy writer, performer and traveller. Says he likes listening to people in pubs and cafés to find out what makes them tick. He often uses his vivid imagination to create humour. Idealistic, quiet, flexible and friendly. Do you share these qualities?

Peter Kay

Talented comedy writer, performer and chart-topper. Energetic, imaginative, warm, generous and hardworking. These qualities make his humour as popular as it is funny and prolific. The realistic characters he creates and shares with us are a combination of his imagination and accurate observation of people. Do you share these qualities?

Richard Branson

One of the most famous and successful British entrepreneurs around. Sociable, visionary, objective and decisive. He is happy to learn from his mistakes, though his analytical mind ensures many a success. Has a go for it/let's-do-it attitude that spreads to those around him. Do you share these qualities?

Bob Geldof

In-your-face musician and campaigner. Will generally say what he believes is true even if it upsets some people. Uses determination, creativity and oral skills to seek out solutions to complex problems. An independent, flexible and analytical mind. Do you share these qualities?

Jonathan Ross

Jack of all trades (except anything practical), interested in finding fun and excitement in everything. An almost childlike sense of curiosity in everything that he finds interesting, but can become quickly bored. Imaginative, enthusiastic, sociable, friendly and adaptable. Do you share these qualities?

Gary Lineker

Mr nice guy. The only professional footballer never to be booked. Popular, friendly, reliable, practical and organised. Likes others to be the same. Usually looks for the best in people. This type of personality tends to be happiest when providing for people, friends or family. Do you share these qualities?

Jeremy Clarkson

TV presenter, writer and lover of fast machines. Will generally offer his opinion even if it is not a popular one! Often has funny and original ideas. Assertive, adventurous, fearless, independent and busy. Do you share these qualities?

Delia Smith

One of the first celebrity chefs and still selling cookbooks by the millions. Also, chair of Norwich City Football Club. Personality strengths include being responsible, focused, quietly determined, realistic, practical, objective, organised and a careful planner. Do you share these qualities?

Shrek

Computer–generated hero of the films named after him. Remember, sharing his personality does not mean you look like him! He is quiet, determined, independent, adaptable and practical, and enjoys his own space and company. Will stand up for what he believes in. Do you share these qualities?

Cinderella

Fairy-tale character with an interesting personality. Quiet, imaginative, caring, devoted and hardworking. Qualities that were exploited by her stepmother and sisters, but ultimately helped her find her true love. Let's hope he treated her a bit better once they were married! Anyway, do you share these qualities?

Ray Mears

Explorer and teacher supreme of bush craft. When you see him on TV, you can't fail to be impressed by his practical, sensible, calm, sensitive qualities. His respect for, and genuine interest in, both the environment he visits and people he is with are inspirational. A quiet, confident explorer. Do you share these qualities?

Lisa Simpson

A young cartoon character with a well-developed personality. Determined, imaginative and focused on solving problems. A clear view of what she wants to achieve, combined with the determination to make her dreams come true, means she is a natural leader. Can observe quietly for a while before giving a considered opinion. Do you share these qualities?

Albert Einstein

Classic mad-professor type of personality! Independent, curious, imaginative, analytical, problem solver. Can 'live in his own head', so absorbed in thinking through problems and puzzles to be solved. Interested in inventing or creating new solutions. Do you share these qualities?

Were you right? Work out your own personality using Pages 12-28, then read your description, see Page 29.

Preferences – what are yours?

Try folding your arms both ways. Now sign your name, first with your preferred hand, then with the other hand. How did it feel?

Preferred way	Other way
easy	hard
natural	had to think
comfortable	uncomfortable
without thinking	really concentrating
cool	rock hard

Some researchers think that cats and dogs are either left-handed or right-handed, but all polar bears are left-handed!

Who are you more like?

E

I

Eddy

I think out loud
I prefer variety and action
I like to act quickly
I'm a good talker
I like to give my opinion

Ian

I think before I speak
I prefer quiet
I like to be careful
I'm a good listener
I keep my thoughts to myself

Remember, both are good. Which is the real you?

So what is your preference: *E* or *I*?

The difference between *E* and *I* preferences is usually the easiest to spot.

E preferences like to talk, discuss, think out loud (they often put their foot in it with their mouth); they tend to flit around from topic to topic while chatting (often not sticking to the point – 'What was I saying?' they may say halfway through a ramble! They are usually people you know a lot about, their favourite film, TV show, food and hobbies, because they tend to talk.

E preferences are more likely to talk to the TV, and perhaps even argue with it! They are also more likely to liven up emails with CAPITAL LETTERS and exclamation marks!!! than *I* preferences.

I preferences tend to think before they speak. They mull it over and give you their considered opinion; they tend to avoid waffle; they are often private and you may not know a lot about them because they tend to give their opinion only when asked for it.

An *E* generally likes to talk about things whereas an *I* doesn't need to.

While delivering a two-day course that ran on a Friday and the following Monday, I gave the group homework that required them to behave in the opposite way to their preference at some point over the weekend. On Monday, Emma asked if she could share what had happened to her. She said she has an *E* preference and her three friends (whom she had been going out with most Friday nights for the past ten years) have *I* preferences.

This Friday, she decided to be quiet and listen rather than do all of the talking. Can you guess what happened? After just a couple of minutes, one of her friends asked if she was OK. She said she was fine and stayed quiet. After two more minutes, all of her friends said they would not say anything more until she told them what was wrong. She told them about her homework. She said she'd found out stuff about her friends she didn't know just by listening for a change, which she thought was amazing, as she'd known them for ten years. Her story also shows how we tend to stay in our preferred letter because people think there's something wrong with us when we're different.

An *I* preference also tried the homework. At a party, he thought he would talk to all ten people in the room before he left. Normally, he'd have spoken to just one person if possible, even after a few pints. He said it was scary and tiring but very exciting. His topic of conversation was the course he was doing and his homework. He found everyone was interested. You could try this

– keep *The Buzz* with you and you can help other people discover their personality preferences.

Getting on better with people

Tips to try out

E/I behaviour is how we interact with the world, our direction of attention – outward (to people or things) or inward (to our own thoughts, feelings). To communicate effectively we need to use the best of both.

E's, you should learn to listen. Do not dominate a conversation. Encourage others to speak and describe their ideas. Don't interrupt or finish people's sentences! Count to five in your head before speaking. It will be tough but *I*'s will be impressed by your listening skills. Learn to put your ideas down in writing. This will help clarify your ideas and appeal to *I*'s. As Stephen Covey once said, first seek to understand, then to be understood.

I's, your written thoughts are usually well thought out and clear. When talking, don't stop when you're interrupted, but politely ask if you can finish your point and say you'll then listen to the other person (it's usually an *E* who interrupts!). *I*'s can help *E*'s by returning them to the point and by not getting annoyed with their 'thinking out loud'.

David and Victoria Beckham on *Parkinson*

Soon after moving to Madrid, Victoria and David Beckham were interviewed on the chat show *Parkinson*.

Parky turned to David and asked if he'd settled in at Real Madrid.

David, an *I* preference, started to think about the question and go inside himself to think about an answer. As he was preparing an answer, Victoria, an *E*, leaned over and said, 'He's settled in very well, Parky. Thanks for asking.' Listen out in conversations and see if you can spot this *E* and *I* difference.

Who are you more like?

S   **N**

Sharon	**Naz**
I look for the facts	I look for the possibilities
I look for details	I like to work out what it means
I focus on what works now	I focus on how to make it different
I prefer using what I've learned	I prefer learning new skills
I'm more practical and sensible	I'm more of a dreamer and imaginative

Remember, both are good. Which is the real you?

So what is your preference: *S* or *N*?

Which behaviour are you more comfortable using? *S* preference is about gathering information by looking for detail. Asking, 'What have we got here?' *S* is generally about being practical, sensible and realistic, knowing what needs to be done, living in the 'present', the real world.

N preference is about exploring beyond the information given, perhaps searching for deeper meaning. Asking, 'How can we change this? What does this mean?' *N* is generally about being imaginative and creative with ideas, living in the 'future'. Both ways of gathering information about the world are useful.

Child's play

From an early age, both my children clearly displayed their *S* and *N* preferences.

My daughter has an *S* preference. When playing, she liked to know what she was supposed to do, how it worked, so she could follow the 'rules' of a jigsaw, train or tea set. Teachers tend to like *S*-preference children who seek to know what the rules are (especially if they then apply the rules J rather than question and challenge *N* or *P*, but we'll get to that later).

We were watching *Teletubbies*. At some points in the programme, we go through a Teletubby's belly and watch a clip of something. This time, we saw a young girl making chocolate Rice Krispies cakes. She was stirring round the melted chocolate over the Rice Krispies. She stopped and looked at the spoon hungrily. She then put it in her mouth and licked off some of the chocolate and quickly put the spoon back in the bowl, hoping no one would notice. At that point, my daughter said to me, 'She shouldn't have done that, Daddy. She should have waited until she'd finished before licking the spoon.' Wow, I thought, an *S* preference.

My son is an *N* preference. When he plays with things, his imagination takes over. A jigsaw becomes the surface of a dangerous planet, while the saucers of my daughter's tea set become meteors that he throws on the surface of the hostile planet. His sister looks on bemused, thinking, 'This is not how you're supposed to do jigsaws or play picnic,' as a cup (now a space rocket to my son) flies just past her head!

To an *N* child, witches and wizards lurk everywhere. When there are loads of 'Why?' questions, there is usually an *N* child asking them.

N-preference children (and *N* parents) tend to enjoy fantasy, imaginative stories and play.

Many comedy programmes have central characters who are flawed. Two *N*'s are Del Boy from *Only Fools and Horses* and David Brent from *The Office* – both have active imaginations but their big ideas rarely pay off.

This reminds us that one preference isn't better than the other. Both are useful in different situations.

Getting on better with people

Tips to try out

S/N behaviour is used whenever we take in new information about something and try to make sense of it.

S behaviour focuses on the facts, and using a step-by-step approach until we find a solution. *N* behaviour focuses on the future, looking forward to how something could be different.

Both are important parts of problem solving. It is best to start with *N* behaviour to identify the longer-term goals, aims and destination. Then use *S* thinking to identify the steps required to get there and any potential obstacles. To get along better, *S*, you should allow *N* to 'daydream'. Consider their ideas fully before dismissing them. *N*, please allow the *S* type to point out the real obstacles and work on solutions together.

Are you accident-prone?

Collecting information before making a decision is useful. *S* preferences can sometimes pay too much attention and *N*'s not enough attention to perceived 'facts'.

For example, 90 per cent of accidents happen in your own home, so a sensible thing to do would be to move in next door! You'd reduce your chance of an accident by 90 per cent. If your neighbour didn't like the idea, you could suggest they move into your house and they'd also be 90 per cent safer.

Information is information; it is how we make sense of it that makes it useful or silly.

'*Reality leaves a lot to the imagination.*'

John Lennon

Look out of the window and tell me what you see

This is a good way to check whether someone has an *S* or *N* preference.

Ask them to look out of a window and describe what they see. An *S*-preference person will describe facts and detail. They'll start to become bored after they've described the physical scene in view. An *N* preference will soon start to describe not what is there but what it could mean and could be. They'll make stories and become more interested once they can start using their imagination.

Try this out. It's great fun being able to predict such an important part of someone's personality just from one simple question.

Who are you more like?

F

T

Frank
I tend to follow my heart
I ask, 'How will it affect people?'
I like pleasing people
Giving praise is more important
I tend to be careful saying things that could upset someone

Tom
I tend to follow my head
I ask, 'Is it the right decision?'
I like rules and principles
Telling how it is is more important
I tend to give and take criticism quite easily

Remember, both are good. Which is the real you?

So what is your preference: *F* or *T*?

This preference is based on how we make decisions. Do we like to make decisions based on pleasing people, wondering how it will affect them and make them feel (*F*), i.e. 'Is that OK with you? Are you sure?'

Or, do we like to make the right decision based on the evidence whether or not some people may not like it (*T*), i.e. 'I don't know why people get upset – I'm just telling them how it is'?

My neighbour is a *T* preference. He likes to tell you what he thinks without needing to understand what you think.

When scraping ice from my car windscreen using my Tesco Clubcard (every little helps – I'd lost the proper scraper), my neighbour came out with some de-icer. 'Here you are. You are stupid, aren't you! Use this de-icer. Keep it.' I thanked him and asked how much it cost. He didn't want to be paid. It was a kind act but he did it in a very *T* way. He also watched me the first time I mowed my lawn. He said, 'If I'd been to the barber's and he'd cut my hair like that, I'd have asked for my money back.'

You usually know exactly where you stand with a *T* preference: they tell it how it is (or how they see it, to be more accurate). Sometimes the truth can hurt but is needed. That talent spotter and judge in such programmes as *Pop Idol* and *The X Factor*, Simon Cowell, is a good example. He is probably doing some people a favour when he says, 'You will never be a singer' – even though it may hurt their feelings.

An *F* preference has a different way of making decisions. To them it is important to consider people's feelings and needs. They often back down in an argument just to keep the peace. They are often called 'nice', 'caring' and sometimes 'a soft touch'. I am an *F* preference – I buy six eggs each week, from a man who delivers to our door, though I don't want or need them. I do it because I don't want to hurt his feelings!

This preference is the only one in which there is a gender difference. Can you guess? More men have *T* and more women have *F* preferences. It is perfectly OK if your preference is not the same as your gender stereotype – this is the case for about one in three people.

Getting on better with people

Tips to try out

F behaviour means making decisions based on people's feelings, thoughts and concerns, picking up on their body language and putting yourself in their shoes. This is useful as you are unlikely to upset someone or ignore their contributions while discussing something with them.

Here's a tip for *F*'s: don't beat about the bush when telling a *T* something. They'll usually appreciate your honesty and can often consider it a sign of weakness if you waffle.

T behaviour focuses on the task or required outcome rather than the person involved. Sometimes this means the person may feel ignored or steamrollered. *T* behaviour is good to keep everyone focused on the task or purpose of the discussion at hand. It removes any thoughts of favouritism or sentimentality. But do also use *F* behaviour to observe each person and check out they understand and can agree with what needs to be done.

Basketball blues

A sports studies student used *The Buzz* to get on better with his best friend. They both play in the same basketball team and are both excellent players.

After each game, John's friend is very critical of his performance, saying he should have done this and that better; this upset John. He realised that he is an *F* preference (takes things personally) and his friend is a *T* preference (gives and takes criticism without getting upset). Now he understands this, he doesn't become annoyed by his friend's comments – they are just different.

Who are you more like?

J   P

Jane
I like to plan and organise things
I like to make decisions
I prefer finishing tasks
I quite like using lists
I like things tidy

Paula
I like to see how
things turn out
I like to keep my options open
I prefer starting tasks
I'd rather not use lists
I don't mind things untidy

Remember, both are good. Which is the real you?

So what is your preference: *J* or *P*?

This chunk of personality is about our attitude to making decisions. Some people prefer to get things done, decide, finish and then move on. They usually like using lists and like to finish things they start (*J*).

Other people prefer to wait and see. They prefer to gather information about things and keep their options open. They generally like to start things more often than finishing them (*P*).

J or *P* preference usually has a big impact on relationships within families, with friends and work/education.

Ask a group of people, (a) 'Do you like to get things sorted and done before you relax?' or (b) 'Can you relax any time?'

What usually happens is *J* – preference people answer (a) and *P* – preference people answer (b). *J* – preference people say they just can't relax until the jobs are done, whereas *P* – preference people can generally leave stuff until later and relax.

There are exceptions to this rule. When I've asked groups of people at work, with their boss present, if they (*J*) like to get their work finished before relaxing or (*P*) can relax any time, most say (*J*)!

When I ask groups of teenagers, they mostly say they can relax any time. This shows the power of peer pressure: at work, to schedule and finish jobs; at school or college, to appear laid back and cool!

Peer pressure can override preference. Our own self-discipline and willpower can also override our preferences. This can be a good thing and a bad thing, depending upon the resulting behaviour.

Our preference should be seen as useful, because it provides clues to our general behaviour, but it is worth remembering that it is good to develop our nonpreference. This behavioural flexibility increases our choice and is covered in later sections of *The Buzz*.

A quiet or noisy car?

Spotting *J* and *P* preferences, in yourself and in others, can be great fun. If you're in someone's car and the only sound you hear as you turn a corner is the tick-tick of the indicator, you can be reasonably sure that the driver is a *J*-preference person. If you're turning a corner in a car and the sound you hear is sweet wrappers, empty drink cans and old magazines shuffling across the back seat, you can be reasonably sure the driver is a *P* preference – unless it's a new car, which *P*'s keep tidy for the first month!

Getting on better with people

Tips to try out

A *J*-behaviour person is a naturally good timekeeper. Managing their own time and sticking to a plan is the way they like to live. Employers like this because the work gets done.

A *P*-preference person generally finds it more difficult to work at a steady pace. They tend to enjoy starting tasks but often get bored or easily distracted and move on to something else. They often complete work at the last minute. Employers tend not to like this approach.

Here's a *P*-preference tip. At the start of a task such as revision, write down what you have to achieve (goals) by the end of the allocated time. Allow yourself flexibility within the achievement of the goals.

Sometimes unexpected things happen, at work and home. This is when a *P* preference is useful. Changing a routine or schedule is easier for a *P* than a *J*. Sometimes *J*'s need to go with the flow. Just because things have always been done a certain way, it does not mean a new approach is the wrong way.

And a *J*-preference tip. Every so often, stop working through your list and ask yourself if you would be better off changing your plan rather than finishing it because you have to, or because you always do it this way.

Garden secrets

Walk past a garden and see the owner's preference. If you see a neat and tidy lawn bordered with alternate red and yellow flowers, spaced equally, of course, you're looking at a *J* garden! You'll also see a bit-of-a-mess garden – that could look good one day when the *P* owner gets round to it – because about half of people have each preference.

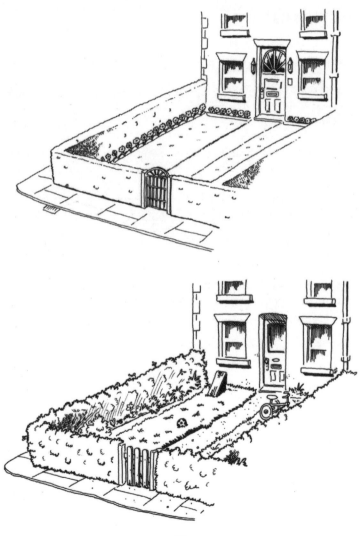

The person who invented outdoor hoovers that suck up leaves and other debris must have been a *J* preference – someone dedicated to tidying up nature (autumn is a messy *P* season)! The inventors of pebbledash and road resurfacing must have been *P* preferences – let's just chuck the stuff on, go home and let it settle down naturally. Perhaps all builders are *P* preference!

Plus or minus?

The fifth chunk of personality is about how we react to situations.

When we are faced with a challenge, we can face in a positive direction by thinking about the positive outcome we would like to achieve, or face in a negative direction, worry about what could go wrong and imagine it.

Look in both directions, but motivation to achieve our best happens when we face in a positive direction.

Some people face in a negative direction for their whole lives – sad, scared, angry, bored, anxious and stressed. They usually blame people or things for being in the direction they are.

A negative direction is usually chosen, not caused. It is a direction, not a place. It is often just a habit – a bad habit. And bad habits can be changed into good ones.

Imagine chewing tinfoil now. Feel the metal cut your tongue as you crunch into it. Or imagine melted chocolate in your mouth, swallow the lovely taste. *Mmm!* You can choose the direction to go.

Some people decide to face in a positive direction.

They usually find themselves in moods such as happy, confident, relaxed and 'go for it'.

Getting on better with people

Tips to try out

To ensure '+' is explored, ask people what they would like to happen. What is the best outcome they could hope for? How can they get there? Who can help them? How will they feel once they've achieved the goal?

To ensure '–' is acknowledged, ask what obstacles are there in the way? What mistakes can we avoid? Once mistakes have been identified, move on to how you can solve them: the '+'.

The fifth chunk of personality

Which statement in each pair do you agree with the more?

I don't take the credit when I do things well	I take the credit when I do things well
I don't know my main strengths and skills	I do know my main strengths and skills
I don't know what I want to achieve from life	I do know what I want to achieve from life
I don't believe in me, yet	I do believe in me, now
I tend to hesitate when opportunities come my way	I tend to go for it

The first statement in each pair sees us pointing in a negative direction. The second statement sees us pointing in a positive direction.

Research has discovered five useful habits for a more positive direction:

- Take the credit when you do things well.
- Know your strengths.
- Know what you want to achieve from life.
- Believe in yourself, now.
- Develop a 'go for it' attitude.

The fifth letter can have an effect on the other eight, as we can see in the next two tables.

Our behaviour when we're pointing in a positive direction:

E	N	F	P
confident	imaginative	friendly	flexible
assertive	creative	caring	open-minded
I	**S**	**T**	**J**
careful	practical	logical	getting things done
being a good listener	realistic	honest	determined

Our behaviour when we're pointing in a negative direction:

E	N	F	P
aggressive	daydreamer	oversensitive to criticism	lazy
loud	unrealistic	talking behind people's backs	never finishing anything
I	**S**	**T**	**J**
unfriendly	nit picking	bossy	fussy
being a loner	predictable	insensitive to people's feelings	boring

Putting your preferences together

1. Check your type with the descriptions of Eddy and Ian, Sharon and Naz, Tom and Frank, Jane and Paula.

2. You should have a combination of the following letters:
   E or I and S or N and T or F and P or J.

3. Once you're satisfied, check out the descriptions based on your four-letter preferences added together:

ISTJ:
Polar bear
Pages 30-1

INFP:
Seal
Pages 40-1

ESFP:
Lion
Pages 52-3

ISFJ:
Koala
bear
Pages 32-3

INTP:
Tawny
owl
Pages 42-3

ENFJ:
Dolphin
Pages 54-5

ISTP:
Tiger
Pages 34-5

INTJ:
Barn owl
Pages 44-5

ENFP:
Clown fish
Pages 56-7

ISFP:
Cat
Pages 36-7

ESTJ:
Black bear
Pages 46-7

ENTP:
Falcon
Pages 58-9

INFJ:
Sea horse
Pages 38-9

ESFJ:
Teddy
bear
Pages 48-9

ENTJ:
Eagle
Pages 60-1

ESTP:
Panther
Pages 50-1

ISTJ: Polar bear

Polar bears are strong and determined. They are at the top of their food chain and, like ISTJs, they can be the boss. To hunt for food, they have to learn and perfect their skills. ISTJs also like to perfect their skills and then use them throughout their life. Polar bears, like ISTJs, can spend a lot of time on their own and be perfectly happy while in their own company.

Strengths

Can work quietly and steadily on something until it is finished.

Like using skills we've already learned.

Good at planning how long a task will take.

Pay attention to details and like to get the job done properly.

Like analysing and putting things into logical order.

Good at organising their own time.

Can make decisions without being soft.

Can follow plans and decide quickly.

As teenagers

Often more adult than the adults! They value their independence, privacy and personal space.

They tend to have a small number of close friends.

Perhaps they could learn to be more sensitive to people while talking to them and sometimes be a little more open to new ideas and new ways of doing things.

They're dependable, loyal and responsible.

As a boyfriend/girlfriend

They're usually more practical, loyal and sensible than romantic and spontaneous. They like stability and structure with clear rules and roles. They'll tell you what they think and expect from the relationship.

When they're pointing in a positive direction

They use their experience to explore problems.

They solve problems in a practical way.

They are careful, sensible, honest and determined.

They learn from their mistakes, have fun.

When they're pointing in a negative direction

They can imagine the worst is going to happen.

They jump to the wrong conclusions.

To reduce stress?

Take a break sometimes and praise people around you.

Your personality buzzwords

Practical, loyal annd reliable.

Fame Academy

FAMOUS EXAMPLES (PROBABLY):

Jeff Tracey (the dad in *Thunderbirds*), Steve Davis (snooker's 'Mr Interesting'), Delia Smith (chair of Norwich City FC and famous chef), Gordon Brown (Chancellor of the Exchequer), Kelly Holmes (athlete), Mr Darcy (from *Bridget Jones's Diary*), Alan Shearer and Michael Owen (footballers).

Preferred learning style

They like quiet for concentration and to work alone.

They like to know the practical benefits before starting.

They like logical order and to be able to show they understand.

They like a clear structure and timetable.

Revision tips

Discuss your work with tutors and friends and be flexible to their ideas to enhance your knowledge base. Don't just stick with working solidly alone.

Preferred roles

Inspector, supervisor, organiser, leader, parent.

Job themes

Organising things (using systems and procedures) appeals, such as financial (accountancy, insurance), uniformed and protective services (police, traffic warden, prison officer, roadside breakdown recovery), environmental services (trading standards, RSPCA inspector), floristry, air-cabin crew, administration, plumber, surveying and law.

Degree-course ideas

Business and management, built environment (architecture, surveying), engineering, law, environmental protection.

Job ideas that don't require loads of qualifications

Postal delivery, shoe/key repair, traffic warden, bricklayer, tiler, car mechanic/fitter, painter and decorator, welder, plumber, driving instructor/examiner.

Delia Smith

One of the first celebrity chefs and still selling cookbooks by the millions. Also, chair of Norwich City Football Club. Personality strengths include being responsible, focused, quietly determined, realistic, practical, objective, organised and a careful planner. Do you share these qualities?

ISFJ: Koala bear

Koala bears are popular and warm animals. Koalas like the safety of their eucalyptus trees; ISFJs like the security and safety of their families, being loyal and caring to those around them. Koalas have strong muscles around their pouch to protect their young; ISFJs can also be strong and determined to protect what they believe in.

Strengths

Can work quietly and steadily on something until it is finished.

Like using skills they've already learned.

Good at planning how a long task will take.

Patient with people and details.

Good at bringing up relevant facts.

Can be aware of other people's beliefs, values and strengths.

Popular team members but rarely push their views forward unless asked.

Can follow plans and decide quickly.

As teenagers

They can be seen as kind and quiet and are popular because they're sensitive to others' needs.

They're realistic, down to earth and respect tradition and authority.

They probably undersell their achievements and can be overlooked.

They could let go a little more and have fun.

As a boyfriend/girlfriend

They're usually loyal, loving and reliable. They go out of their way to support their partner. Sometimes they can be too nice for their own good.

When they're pointing in a positive direction

They use experience to explore problems, then solve them in a practical way, taking into account the feelings of people.

They're good listeners, practical, honest, get things done.

They learn from their mistakes, have fun.

When they're pointing in a negative direction

They imagine the worst is going to happen and can jump to the wrong conclusions.

To reduce stress?

Can sometimes be too nice? Stick up for yourself!

Your personality buzzwords

Practical, modest and caring.

Fame Academy

FAMOUS EXAMPLES (PROBABLY):

Marge Simpson (loyal, homemaker from *The Simpsons*), David Beckham (footballer, former England captain, dedicated, quiet and determined), Mother Teresa (helped the poor in Calcutta), Will Young (surprise *Pop Idol* winner who can write and sing very well).

Preferred learning style

They like quiet for concentration and to work alone.

They like to know 'Why?' and 'What for?' before doing.

They like to be praised and encouraged.

They like structure, procedures and finishing times to be clear.

Revision tips

They're generally very good at revising, but take breaks now and again; also check with your tutors that your schedule is OK.

Preferred roles

Protector, inspector, organiser, provider, carer

Job themes

Jobs in which they can use their organisational skills without fuss and fanfare: business/administration, public sector, health service, library/information work, caring (for individuals), financial services, fire/ambulance service, hairdressing/beauty, dental work, electrician. They like to learn how to do a job, and then do it well.

Degree-course ideas

Medical therapies (speech, occupational, physiotherapy), nursing, business studies, library/information, science, primary-school teaching, law.

Job ideas that don't require loads of qualifications

Care worker, call-centre worker, stagehand, office worker, cleaner, sports massage, waiter/waitress, retail assistant, teaching assistant, childcare worker.

David Beckham

Famous footballer and former England captain who is naturally talented but is also prepared to practise long hours to be the best footballer he can be. Quiet, friendly, down-to-earth, organised, determined, reliable, caring and hardworking. Do you share these qualities?

ISTP: Tiger

Tigers are rare, as are ISTPs. Although there are only five species left, they are determined and strong, like ISTPs. They are the largest cat and can be confident and assertive explorers, enjoying finding out about the world around them, like ISTPs.

Strengths

Can work quietly and steadily on a number of things at once.

Like using skills they've already learned.

Can look at situations and make decisions without getting upset.

Can organise the facts carefully.

Can stand up for what they believe in, even if others don't agree.

Can be flexible and try new ways to get things done.

Can be patient with routine.

As teenagers

They're honest and realistic with great common sense and a love for life.

If someone doesn't make sense, they'll tell them so. This can sometimes make them seem stubborn and strong-willed.

They could try to take into account the personal needs and feelings of friends and family – criticise only when they really need to.

As a boyfriend/girlfriend

They're usually good fun to be with, though may sometimes be too honest with their opinions for their own good.

When they're pointing in a positive direction

They are good at analysing situations and stand up for what they believe in.

They are good listeners, practical, logical, flexible.

They learn from their mistakes, have fun.

When they're pointing in a negative direction

They have emotional outbursts and mood swings.

They argue over tiny details.

To reduce stress?

Share your good ideas and humour around.

Your personality buzzwords

Independent, analytical and determined.

Fame Academy

FAMOUS EXAMPLES (PROBABLY):

Ellen MacArthur, Clint Eastwood, Shrek and Tom Cruise – quiet, curious, determined and adaptable!

Preferred learning style

They like quiet for concentration and can work well alone.

They like to know what the practical benefits will be before starting.

They like a logical order, to know what they're supposed to do, but not how to do it (they'll work out their own way).

Revision tips

They tend to prefer practical, hands-on learning and may try to get away with the bare minimum on assignments. They could learn themselves, not leaving things to the last minute.

Preferred roles

Explorer, firefighter, performer, operator.

Job themes

Satisfying enjoyable work rather than a 'career' usually appeals.

Agriculture, horticulture, forestry, environmental work, engineering and crafts can provide satisfaction. Law, Armed forces, legal work, transport manager, trading standards, TV camera operator, wildlife photographer.

Degree-course ideas

Ecology, biological sciences, agriculture/ horticulture, geography, geology, engineering, built environment (surveying, town planning, landscape architecture).

Job ideas that don't require loads of qualifications

Bus/taxi driver, roofer, refuse collector, toolmaker, garden-centre worker, car mechanic/fitter, tiler, farm worker, roadie, warehouse worker, windscreen repairer/ fitter, construction crafts.

Shrek

Computer–generated hero of the films named after him. Remember, sharing his personality does not mean you look like him! He is quiet, determined, independent, adaptable and practical, and enjoys his own space and company. Will stand up for what he believes in. Do you share these qualities?

ISFP: Cat

Domestic cats, like ISFPs, are popular and friendly despite spending a lot of time on their own. Kittens climb trees. In 1950, a four-month-old kitten climbed to the top of a mountain in the Alps. ISFPs also tend to like exploring the outdoors.

Strengths

Can work quietly and steadily on a number of things at once.

Like using skills they've already learned.

Can enjoy what's going on now.

Can adapt and change their plans.

Can be aware of people's strengths and beliefs.

Are popular team members but rarely push their views forward unless asked.

Can be sympathetic.

Can be careful with their facts.

As teenagers

They have an eye for quality and often have collections. They're often very close to their family and can feel nervous about leaving home.

They could learn that sometimes they just need to make a decision, though it may upset some people!

They're loyal friends, good at solving problems.

As a boyfriend/girlfriend

They're usually good fun to be with, though often like time on their own to recharge their batteries. They enjoy sharing activities, such as hobbies, with their partner that get them out and about.

When they're pointing in a positive direction

They are good at making people feel included and valued.

They are good listeners, practical, caring, open-minded.

They learn from their mistakes, have fun.

When they're pointing in a negative direction

They criticise and become stubborn.

To reduce stress?

Try finishing nearly as many things as you start!

Your personality buzzwords

Independent, analytical and determined.

Fame Academy

FAMOUS EXAMPLES (PROBABLY):

Sir Paul McCartney, Ray Mears (explorer), Bill Oddie (TV nature presenter), Marilyn Monroe and Mozart – friendly, artistic, succeeding when they trust their inner voice.

Preferred learning style

They like quiet for concentration and can work alone.

They like to know the practical benefits before starting.

They like praise, encouragement and flexibility.

Revision tips

Motivate yourself with treats and rewards for finishing revision and coursework.

Don't be afraid to learn new things and ways of doing things. Practice makes perfect.

Preferred roles

Performer, promoter, improviser, carer

Job themes

Practical service to people, e.g. hospitality, retail, caring work.

Many love animals, and work with animals can be rewarding for them, e.g. RSPCA inspector.

Agriculture, forestry (environment), farming, floristry and horticulture careers can also appear, as can youth work.

Creative roles often appeal: art, craft or music.

Degree-course ideas

Ecology, agriculture/horticulture, built environment (surveying, architecture, planning).

Job ideas that don't require loads of qualifications

Bus/taxi/van driver, sports massage, roofer, care worker, tree surgeon, farm worker, working with animals (kennels, pet shops), milk-deliverer, horticultural worker, ranger/warden (wildlife/environment), musician/DJ.

Ray Mears

Explorer and teacher supreme of bush craft. When you see him on TV, you can't fail to be impressed by his practical, sensible, calm, sensitive qualities. His respect for, and genuine interest in, both the environment he visits and people he is with are inspirational. A quiet, confident explorer. Do you share these qualities?

INFJ: Sea horse

Sea horses have been credited with deep magical qualities. INFJs can also be deep, quiet and imaginative. Sea horses tend to live in warm waters and care for their young; INFJs can be warm and caring. The head shape of a sea horse is as unique as a human fingerprint and INFJs value their own and other's uniqueness.

Strengths

Can work quietly on something until it is finished.

Interested in the idea behind what they're doing, especially how it affects people.

Patient with complicated situations.

Solve problems using their imagination.

Can be aware of people's values and strengths.

Can persuade others.

Can follow plans.

Can decide quickly.

As teenagers

At their best they can inspire others!

They're usually good students and enjoy academic activity, but can be hard to get to know.

They can be perfectionists and they like to please others.

This sometimes means they put more pressure on ourselves than they need to.

They can be their own hardest critics!

As a boyfriend/girlfriend

They're usually romantic and caring and like the same from their partner. They usually come across as deep and intense but can be very funny when they want to be.

When they're pointing in a positive direction

They solve problems with imagination and enthusiasm.

They are good listeners, creative and caring, and get things done.

They learn from their mistakes, have fun.

When they're pointing in a negative direction

They become easily annoyed and angry.

They can overeat, drink too much or do too much exercise.

To reduce stress?

Don't just live inside your head – talk to others, share more of your great ideas.

Your personality buzzwords

Modest, caring and loyal.

Fame Academy

FAMOUS EXAMPLES (PROBABLY):

Victoria Wood, Gandhi, Cinderella and Velma (from *Scooby Doo*) – strong inner beliefs combined with determination and warmth.

Preferred learning style

They like quiet for concentration.

They like to know the theory behind the idea.

They like encouragement and praise.

They like structure, procedures and to know finishing times.

Revision tips

Usually good at revising and completing course work.

Don't ignore practical details and considerations.

Motivate yourself by imagining the positive benefits all your hard work could bring – but then make sure you get on with the work!

Preferred roles

Counsellor, adviser, healer, mentor.

Job themes

Supporting individuals to be their best, such as through caring work, social work, counselling, advising, psychology, advocacy, medical therapies.

Library/information work, languages, archaeology, creative writing, journalism, marketing, science (life/physical).

Degree-course ideas

Psychology, history, languages, linguistics, social/life sciences.

Job ideas that don't require loads of qualifications

Youth worker, hotel porter, hairdresser, picture framer, care worker, display designer, waiter/waitress, sports massage, tattooist, business administrator, library/teaching assistant, secretary/receptionist.

Cinderella

Fairy-tale character with an interesting personality. Quiet, imaginative, caring, devoted and hardworking. Qualities that were exploited by her stepmother and sisters, but ultimately helped her find her true love. Let's hope he treated her a bit better once they were married! Anyway, do you share these qualities?

INFP: Seal

Seals can be imaginative, supportive and playful around their social group, as can INFPs. They can also be quiet and careful on land, and INFPs can share this deeper, more watchful behaviour, wondering whether to jump in and trust their instincts or suss out the person or situation first.

Strengths

Can work quietly and steadily on a number of things at once.

Enjoy learning new skills.

Are full of enthusiasm.

Are interested in the thinking behind the idea, particularly how it affects people.

Solve problems using their imagination.

Can be aware of people's strengths and values.

Can persuade others.

Can adapt and change their plans.

Can work on many things at once.

As teenagers

They have strong inner values and beliefs that they like to live by – others can therefore see them as sensitive, complex and deep.

They tend to have close relationships with a few rather than a wide circle of friends.

They naturally dislike rules – though sometimes these could help them!

As a boyfriend/girlfriend

They're usually romantic and loving and expect the same from their partner. Can be funny. Can be very sensitive to criticism so be careful how you deliver it.

When they're pointing in a positive direction

They are good at making people feel valued and included.

They are good listeners, imaginative, caring, flexible.

They learn from their mistakes, have fun.

When they're pointing in a negative direction

They can criticise and become stubborn.

To reduce stress?

Don't get lost inside your head – share some of your good ideas with others.

Your personality buzzwords

Friendly, modest and imaginative.

Fame Academy

FAMOUS EXAMPLES (PROBABLY):

Shakespeare, Michael Palin (well-travelled *Python*), ET (probably the cutest extraterrestrial to visit Earth) and Julia Roberts (actress) – all sharing strong principles to understand and support people!

Preferred learning style

They like quiet for concentration.

They like to know the theory behind the idea.

They like to be encouraged and praised.

They like variety and choices.

Revision tips

Can get lost in their own heads sometimes! Think of a practical plan to make sure there is enough time to finish everything.

They generally take criticism very personally – but remember that some criticism could help improve future work!

Preferred roles

Counsellor, adviser, mentor, advocate.

Job themes

Interested in possibilities for people – attracted to counselling, advising, psychology, advocating, mentoring and medical therapies.

Also interested in written expression – library/information work, journalism, research and archaeology, art and creative work.

Degree-course ideas

Psychology, languages, linguistics, history, politics, social sciences.

Job ideas that don't require loads of qualifications

Sports/remedial massage, alternative therapist (aromatherapy, reiki, reflexology, neurolinguistic programming (NLP), picture framer, care worker, photographer, counsellor adviser (marriage guidance, debt), youth worker, care assistant.

Michael Palin

Famous comedy writer, performer and traveller. Says he likes listening to people in pubs and cafés to find out what makes them tick. He often uses his vivid imagination to create humour. Idealistic, quiet, flexible and friendly. Do you share these qualities?

INTP: Tawny owl

Owls are symbols of intelligence, determination and wisdom – qualities usually shared with INTPs. They fly silently in the night, and INTPs, too, are often careful and quiet, speaking only when they have something interesting or useful to say. If you hear an owl hoot at night, it is likely to be a tawny owl, and, when you hear an INTP speak; it is usually worth listening to.

Tawny owls are Britain's most common bird of prey, but INTPs are quite rare and therefore easy to misunderstand.

Strengths

Can work quietly and steadily on a number of things at once.

Enjoy learning new skills.

Enjoy solving problems using their imagination.

Like analysing and putting things in logical order.

Interested in the theory behind the idea, particularly theories that can be tested and proved.

Can adapt and change their plans.

Can be careful with details.

As teenagers

They're independent, quiet and flexible deep thinkers.

They don't suffer fools gladly and can annoy people who might think they're cold, but they're more interested in the core issues, and they're their own harshest critics at times.

Perhaps they could show more appreciation of others input and the practical details to make sure things run smoothly.

As a boyfriend/girlfriend

They usually share their ideas, passions and beliefs. They like trying new things together. They can be very self-critical.

When they're pointing in a positive direction

They are good at analysing situations and stand up for what they believe in.

They're good listeners, imaginative, logical, flexible, learn from their mistakes, have fun.

When they're pointing in a negative direction

They have emotional outbursts and mood swings.

They argue over tiny details.

To reduce stress?

If you're not sure what people are thinking, ask!

Your personality buzzwords

Fame Academy

FAMOUS EXAMPLES (PROBABLY):

Caractacus Potts (from *Chitty Chitty Bang Bang*), Albert Einstein, Wallace (from *Wallace and Gromit*) and Sir Isaac Newton – natural inventors!

Preferred learning style

They like quiet for concentration and can work alone.

They like to know the theory behind the idea.

They like a logical order but appreciate being able to decide on their own way to do things.

Revision tips

Concentrate on practical details and finish one thing before moving on to a new challenge.

Plan so you have enough time to get everything done.

Preferred roles

Inventor, architect, creator, engineer.

Job themes

Jobs in which they can organise ideas appeal, considering possibilities and exploring the possible effects.

Computing (web design, software design), architecture, research, law, engineering, surveying and science appeal to an interest in solving technical problems.

Degree-course ideas

Engineering, built environment (surveying, town planning/design, architecture), biotechnology, pure science, computing/IT.

Job ideas that don't require loads of qualifications

Website/IT designer, technician, props maker, stonemason, photographer, signwriter, laboratory assistant/researcher, car mechanic, fixing/repairing stuff, inventor!

Albert Einstein

Classic mad-professor type of personality! Independent, curious, imaginative, analytical, problem solver. Can 'live in his own head', so absorbed in thinking through problems and puzzles to be solved. Interested in inventing or creating new solutions. Do you share these qualities?

INTJ: Barn owl

Owls are symbols of intelligence, determination and wisdom; qualities usually shared with the INTJ. A barn owl hunts quietly over grassland looking for small animals. INTJs can seem to be flying high, thinking big ideas quietly, while paying attention to the small details to solve problems and develop plans.

Strengths

Can be careful with facts.

Can work on something for a long time.

Interested in the idea behind the task.

Like solving problems.

Can be good organisers.

Enjoy learning new skills.

Are patient with complicated situations.

Can be imaginative problem solvers.

Like putting things into a logical order.

Can follow plans and decide quickly.

As teenagers

At their best, they're clever, creative visionaries with the determination to achieve their goals, which means they may be considered aloof, private and argumentative.

They could learn to argue over only the most important things and try to consider others' feelings.

They tend to push at boundaries and rules forced upon them.

They're proud of their competence and don't like to be fussed over.

As a boyfriend/girlfriend

They're usually quite independent but can appear tougher than they really are. They usually like to share their passions, ideas and beliefs.

When they're pointing in a positive direction

They solve problems with imagination and enthusiasm.

They are good listeners, creative, logical, determined.

They learn from their mistakes, have fun.

When they're pointing in a negative direction

They become easily annoyed and angry.

They can overeat, drink too much or do too much exercise.

To reduce stress?

Forgive yourself for not always reaching your really high standards.

Your personality buzzwords

Achiever, reliable and analytical.

Fame Academy

FAMOUS EXAMPLES (PROBABLY):

Thomas Edison, Nick Park (creator of *Wallace and Gromit*), George Lucas (*Star Wars*), Willy Wonka, Gandalf (*Lord of the Rings*), Morrissey and Lisa Simpson – determined and imaginative with strong principles.

Preferred learning style

They like quiet for concentration and can work alone.

They like to know the theory behind the idea before starting.

They like a logical order and to be able to show they understand.

They like a clear structure and timetable.

Revision tips

Because they're good making quick decisions, they may be tempted to skip sections of work, so be careful not to miss important stuff if you're going to do this.

Take time to research and make sure you have a broad understanding of the whole subject.

Preferred roles

Inventor, organiser, strategist, engineer.

Job themes

Organising and managing ideas and information rather than people.

Computer, IT, patent work, engineering, science, library/information work, surveying, market research.

Degree-course ideas

Engineering (structural: bridges, roads and machines), built environment (planning and design), pure science, biotechnology, business/law/economics.

Job ideas that don't require loads of qualifications

Car mechanic/tyre fitter, dental hygienist, IT/website designer, engraver, welder, telephone helpline worker (technical support), health-service technician, politician, business/administrator, self-employment.

Lisa Simpson

A young cartoon character with a well-developed personality. Determined, imaginative and focused on solving problems. A clear view of what she wants to achieve, combined with the determination to make her dreams come true, means she is a natural leader. Can observe quietly for a while before giving a considered opinion. Do you share these qualities?

ESTJ: Black bear

The bear is a symbol of strength and power and ESTJs can be strong, taking charge of situations and organising so that things get done. The black bear is found in the USA, and ESTJs share the no-nonsense, go for it qualities often linked with Americans.

Strengths

Like action.

Can focus on outcomes and results.

Like to use skills they've already learned.

Can act and communicate quickly and decisively.

Are reliable and realistic.

Can stand firm against opposition.

Can make decisions without being seen as soft.

Can organise facts and people using clear thinking.

Can be careful with details.

As teenagers

They're normally in control and in charge. They work out what needs to be done, how it should be done, and then do it!

Some people may get upset with their directness but they usually get things done before considering 'feelings'.

They like to do things for a practical purpose.

Perhaps they should sometimes be more sensitive to people's needs and not stick too much to the details.

They're good at taking charge, which is useful in lots of situations such as emergencies.

As a boyfriend/girlfriend

They usually like to be in charge. They like to know where they stand, what roles and duties they have. They tend to see relationships as a partnership. They can be very loyal and dependable.

When they're pointing in a positive direction

They are good at working out what's going on.

They stand up for what they believe in.

They are confident, realistic, logical, determined.

They learn from mistakes and are fun to be with.

When they're pointing in a negative direction

They are bossy and take criticism very personally.

To reduce stress?

You don't need to take charge all of the time – let others discover solutions.

Your personality buzzwords

Loyal, achiever and determined.

Fame Academy

FAMOUS EXAMPLES (PROBABLY):

The McDonald brothers, who built an empire of fast-food burger bars by developing a clear plan, then delivering it!

Joan Rivers, Katie Price (Jordan), Victoria Beckham, Dr Gillian McKeith (*You Are What You Eat*) and Fred (from *Scooby Doo*) – determined and ambitious, working hard to achieve their goals in a no-nonsense kind of way.

Preferred learning style

They like group activity and discussion.

They like to know the practical benefits before starting.

They like a logical order and clear structure.

Revision tips

Convince yourself of the value and benefits of revising, and you'll do it!

Talk to others to discover new insights.

Preferred roles

Supervisor, inspector, leader, protector.

Job themes

Jobs requiring tasks to be completed with quick results – business management, engineering, dentistry, systems analyst, law, emergency services (police, fire and ambulance).

Self-employment.

Degree-course ideas

Business and management (general: human resources, marketing, accountancy; sector-specific: retail, transport, hotel), law, primary-school teaching.

Job ideas that don't require loads of qualifications

Market trader, van driver, ranger/warden, post-deliverer, stunt performer, window cleaner, painter and decorator, plumber, floor layer, paramedic, sales person, self-employment.

Victoria Beckham

When she was younger, she is said to have stated that her ambition was to become a brand as famous as Nike or Daz. She has certainly achieved this goal by using her knowledge of how the media and business work to full effect. She is determined, confident and hardworking to make the most of her talents. An achiever who gets things done. Do you share these qualities?

ESFJ: Teddy bear

Teddy bears are warm and friendly – qualities usually found in ESFJs. Teddy Bears are often loyal, organised and a bit of a chatterbox – characteristic qualities usually found in ESFJs.

Teddy bears are popular and widespread, as are ESFJs.

Strengths

Friendly, good communicators.

Enjoy applying skills and knowledge they've already learned.

Usually respect traditions, anniversaries and rules.

Can be popular team members.

Can act and communicate quickly and without fuss.

Can be good organisers of people.

Can be patient with detail.

Often know what is going on and join in keeping everyone else involved.

As teenagers

They can be modest about their achievements and be surprised at how well they're liked by friends.

Loyal and realistic, they'll get things done on time.

They can take criticism to heart and sometimes try to please others while forgetting about their own needs.

They work well in teams and people often turn to them for support and help.

They keep their stubborn streak only for those close to them!

As a boyfriend/girlfriend

They're usually very loyal, loving, supportive and protective. They provide stability and structure and are friendly and sociable. They like to spend time with groups of friends and family, not just their partner.

When they're pointing in a positive direction

They are good at making people feel valued and important.

They are assertive, practical, friendly, get things done.

They learn from their mistakes, have fun.

When they're pointing in a negative direction

They take over, saying, 'Oh, I'll do it!'

Dig their heels in.

To reduce stress?

Don't try to be perfect all of the time – chill!

Your personality buzzwords

Friendly, reliable and loyal.

Fame Academy

FAMOUS EXAMPLES (PROBABLY):

Fiona Phillips (*GMTV* presenter), Mary
Poppins, Wendy (*Peter Pan*), Truly
Scrumptious (*Chitty Chitty Bang Bang*),
Gary Lineker, Bones (*Star Trek*), Wonder
Woman (TV character from the 1970s)
– loyal, friendly and chatty.

Preferred learning style

They like group activity and discussion.
They like to know the practical benefits
before starting.
They like praise and encouragement.
They like a clear structure.

Revision tips

Comfortable with routine and detail, so
normally complete revision on schedule.

Try to use and develop your imagination.

Discussing topics with others could help
you expand your knowledge beyond the
textbooks.

Preferred roles

Protector, organiser, provider, supervisor,
carer.

Job themes

Jobs in which they can provide a service
to others using their friendliness and
organisational skills appeal.

Health service (nurse, occupational/speech
therapy), administration, hospitality,
tourism, caring and advice work, teaching,
library/information work, PR and
marketing.

Degree-course ideas

Nursing and medical therapies
(occupational, speech and physiotherapy),
complementary medicine, primary-school
teaching, business services (hospitality
management, conference organising, human
resources, customer service).

Job ideas that don't require loads of qualifications

Care worker, stage hand, call-centre
worker, retail assistant, theme-park worker,
hairdresser/beauty therapist, chef/cook,
waiter/waitress, hotel porter, travel agency
worker, public services worker.

Gary Lineker

Mr nice guy. The only professional footballer never to be booked. Popular, friendly, reliable,
practical and organised. Likes others to be the same. Usually looks for the best in people. This
type of personality tends to be happiest when providing for people, friends or family.

ESTP: Panther

The panther is a confident, fearless explorer, testing its skills in the jungle. These are usually qualities found in ESTPs. Both prefer action and variety. Can be fun to be with, but can bite (usually with a funny comment!) if things get boring.

Strengths

Good at on-the-spot problem solving.

Can act and communicate quickly and decisively.

Like using skills they've already learned.

Can look at situations without becoming easily upset.

Can stand up for what they believe in even if others disagree.

Can adapt and change plans.

Can make decisions without being seen as soft.

Can organise facts.

As teenagers

They enjoy freedom and adventure, which can result in clashes with authority.

They can be risk takers and practical jokers.

They can appear messy and disorganised but they know where their stuff is!

They can be popular because they are fun and easy to be with, though they may sometimes be drawn to the wrong people!

Others often tell them to slow down!

As a boyfriend/girlfriend

They're usually good fun to be with. They're full of energy and ideas. They can be determined and easily become bored – so variety and action keep them happy.

When they're pointing in a positive direction

They use experience to analyse problems, then solve them in a practical way.

They are confident, realistic, logical and flexible.

They learn from their mistakes, have fun.

When they're pointing in a negative direction

They get confused about how they feel and have big ideas, but are unsure how to make them happen.

To reduce stress?

Plan more and your projects can be even more successful.

Your personality buzzwords

Flexible, enthusiastic and determined.

Fame Academy

FAMOUS EXAMPLES (PROBABLY):

Peter Pan, Jeremy Clarkson, Tigger, Zorro, Madonna, James Bond, Bart Simpson, Paul McKenna, Winston Churchill – all objective, determined and impulsive problem solvers!

Preferred learning style

They like group activity, discussion and role play.

They like to know the practical benefits before starting.

They like to know what they're supposed to do but not how to do it (they'll work that out themselves!).

Revision tips

They can become bored with long explanations and theories – they're usually better working with things they can take apart or put together.

Preferred roles

Crafter, performer, promoter, engineer, explorer.

Job themes

Good at solving practical problems on the spot, engineering, science, protecting people and property, IT, surveying, hospitality management, oil and gas production, repair and servicing, law, armed services and environmental careers.

Degree-course ideas

Engineering (structures – roads, bridges, dams and machines), geography, built environment (architect, planner, surveyor, design), ecology, performing arts.

Job ideas that don't require loads of qualifications

Paramedic, scaffolder, van driver, car mechanic, bricklayer, warehouse worker, window cleaner, bingo caller, youth worker, roofer, taxi driver, theme-park worker, construction/engineering crafter.

Jeremy Clarkson

TV presenter, writer and lover of fast machines. Will generally offer his opinion even if it is not a popular one! Often has funny and original ideas. Assertive, adventurous, fearless, independent and busy. Do you share these qualities?

ESFP: Lion

Lions are very sociable cats. They enjoy being with their families and relatives. ESFPs share this interest in socialising and having fun as a way to be close to their loved ones. Lions are graceful and skilful when hunting and ESFPs are often the same in sport or leisure activities that interest them.

Strengths

Friendly, good communicators.

Enjoy using skills already learned.

Can bring up useful facts.

Are good at knowing what's going on.

Can join in with people with enthusiasm.

Can be generous and popular team members.

Are expedient (can adapt and change plans).

Can work on a number of things at once.

As teenagers

They're usually popular and enthusiastic with a zest for life. They dislike routine and conflict – they may try to please everyone, which is difficult all of the time.

They can be very generous with their time and money.

They should try to take criticism less personally – sometimes it can be useful.

They can be real party animals!

As a boyfriend/girlfriend

They're usually great fun to be with. They enjoy being with groups of people, not just on their own with their partner. They enjoy socialising. They can be generous with their time and money.

When they're pointing in a positive direction

They use experience to explore problems, then solve them in a practical way, taking into account the feelings of people.

They are confident, practical, friendly and flexible.

They learn from their mistakes, are fun and exuberant.

When they're pointing in a negative direction

They can get confused about how they feel and have big ideas but are unsure how to make them happen.

To reduce stress?

Don't play all of the time – recharge your batteries.

Your personality buzzwords

Generous, caring and flexible.

Fame Academy

FAMOUS EXAMPLES (PROBABLY):

Elvis, Baloo (from *The Jungle Book*), Bridget Jones, Ant and Dec, Donkey (from *Shrek*), Pinocchio, Homer Simpson, Freddie Flintoff, Ian Botham, Jimmy White – generally 'party' people focused on enjoying the present! Natural performers.

Preferred learning style

They like group activity and discussion.

They like to know the practical benefits before starting.

They like praise and encouragement.

They like variety and action.

Revision tips

Focus on one thing at a time and complete it. Examine the 'bigger picture' and explore your creative-thinking side.

Generally learn well in group discussion (if you can stick to work!).

Preferred roles

Performer, carer, promoter.

Job themes

Jobs in which they can use their natural affinity with people to solve practical immediate problems.

Social and service-oriented, e.g. care work, advice, counselling, medical therapies, retail, estate agency, journalism, hospitality management, administration and tourism.

Practical solutions, e.g. armed forces, quarry/mining, environmental services.

Degree-course ideas

Social sciences, sociology, criminology, retail/hospitality management, history, sport, performing arts.

Job ideas that don't require loads of qualifications

Care worker, scaffolder, refuse collector, taxi driver, chef/cook, van driver, theme-park worker, hotel porter, paramedic, bar person, retail assistant, youth worker, construction crafter.

Bridget Jones

Famous from the film/novel *Bridget Jones's Diary*. Usually says what she's thinking; resulting in embarrassment. She gets away with it because she is fun-loving, enthusiastic, generous and caring. A bit disorganised, but her heart is in the right place. Do you share these qualities?

ENFJ: Dolphin

Many people say the dolphin is their favourite animal, and ENFJs can be very popular too. Both usually share the qualities of intelligence, warmth, great vision and charisma. Dolphins can swim up to 32 kilometres or so (about 20 miles) an hour and sleep only in seven-minute naps. Like dolphins, ENFJs often need to move fast to fit everything in, often enjoying busy and complicated social lives.

Strengths

Friendly, popular, good communicators.

Enjoy learning new skills.

Interested in how ideas affect people.

Can like variety and action.

Can be aware of people's values and principles.

Can focus on getting the job done.

Can be imaginative, creative problem solvers.

As teenagers

They're usually popular, cooperative and friendly. People like their enthusiasm, warmth and compassion.

They can try to keep everyone happy too much and neglect their own needs.

They can jump from one thing to the next without settling on something and doing it really well. They should learn to stay positive, since they can't know everything! And they can say no to people sometimes!

As a boyfriend/girlfriend

They're usually friendly, caring and loving. They work hard at making their relationships strong, deep and meaningful.

When they're pointing in a positive direction

They are good at making people feel valued and important.

They are assertive, creative, friendly and flexible.

They learn from their mistakes, have fun.

When they're pointing in a negative direction

They take over, saying, 'Leave it to me!'

They dig their heels in.

To reduce stress?

Keep some time for yourself. You can't help all of the people all of the time.

Your personality buzzwords

Friendly, generous and imaginative.

Fame Academy

FAMOUS EXAMPLES (PROBABLY):

Martin Luther King, Stephen Fry, Peter Ustinov, Sean Connery, Johnny Depp, Rose Tyler (the Doctor's companion from *Doctor Who*) and Peter Kay – charismatic people we like to listen to.

Preferred learning style

They like group activity and discussion.

They like to know the theory behind the idea.

They like encouragement and praise.

They like structure, procedures and to know finishing times.

Revision tips

Talk about your work with tutors and friends – you usually learn better this way, but find time for private study also.

Focus on the positives and the facts.

Make time for rest and relaxation.

Preferred roles

Counsellor, healer, adviser, advocate, mentor, friend.

Job themes

Jobs in which you can use your people skills to develop ideas and people in an organised way.

Journalism, writer, media, law, teacher, marketing, PR, social science, psychology, medical therapies, management (human resources).

Degree-course ideas

Psychology, law, performing arts, English, linguistics, languages, communications, media, journalism, marketing, advertising, public relations, medical sciences.

Job ideas that don't require loads of qualifications

Coach/trainer, retail assistant, bingo caller, teaching assistant, paramedic, youth worker, tour guide, travel agency worker, conference/hospitality worker, advice worker, carer, holiday centre worker.

Peter Kay

Talented comedy writer, performer and chart-topper. Energetic, imaginative, warm, generous and hardworking. These qualities make his humour as popular as it is funny and prolific. The realistic characters he creates and shares with us are a combination of his imagination and accurate observation of people. Do you share these qualities?

ENFP: Clown fish

Clown fish are energetic, creative and busy fish, and ENFPs usually share these qualities. Clown fish live among anemones but don't feel their stings due to a clever coating on their skin. ENFPs, too, are often thinking of new and clever ways of doing things, preferring variety and action to peace and quiet.

Strengths

Can get things done at the last minute.

Can work on a number of things at once.

Can adapt and change plans.

Are full of enthusiasm.

Can persuade others.

Can solve problems using imagination and improvisation.

Are interested in the idea behind the job, particularly how it affects people.

Enjoy learning new skills.

Can enjoy variety and action.

As teenagers

They make loyal friends.

They're searching for their individual identity, drawn to express themselves through drama, words or art. They don't like being told what to do – they'd rather work that out for themselves.

They can get bored quickly and move on to something new, leaving other things unfinished – which can annoy others. If they were a little more organised, they'd save themselves time and trouble.

They're great at coming up with ideas – especially for others to carry out. Prone to forgetting/losing things – their catchphrase could be, 'Where did I put it?'

As a boyfriend/girlfriend

They're usually fun to be with. They're romantic and also like their partners to be romantic. Because they're easily bored and distracted, novelty and surprise are welcomed.

When they're pointing in a positive direction

They solve problems using imagination and enthusiasm.

They are confident, creative, friendly, flexible.

They learn from their mistakes, have fun.

When they're pointing in a negative direction

They worry about their health, become quiet and sad.

They feel trapped.

To reduce stress?

Take a break sometimes, switch off your brain and chill!

Your personality buzzwords

Imaginative, enthusiastic and flexible.

Fame Academy

FAMOUS EXAMPLES (PROBABLY):

The Cat in the Hat, The Little Mermaid, Jonathan Ross, Terry Wogan, Eamonn Holmes, Anita Roddick, Paul O'Grady, Jamie Oliver – intuitive, enthusiastic and witty dreamers!

Preferred learning style

They like group activity and discussion.

They like to know the theory behind the idea.

They like to be encouraged and praised.

They like variety and choices.

Revision tips

Try to finish something before moving on to the next topic.

Revise in different locations and at different times to add variety.

Imagine completing your revision as a happy way to pass time.

Preferred roles

Counsellor, healer, mentor, adviser, carer, catalyst.

Job themes

Jobs where they can use their imagination, particularly to understand and develop people in a laid-back environment – journalism, psychology, marketing, advertising, speech therapy, teaching, counselling, personnel, training, science (biology/social), performing (arts/music/drama), advice worker.

Degree-course ideas

Psychology, complementary health, secondary teaching, English literature, languages, communication, media, journalism, performing arts.

Job ideas that don't require loads of qualifications

Holiday centre worker, sports massage/therapy, coach/trainer, paramedic, care worker, chef/cook, alternative/complementary health practitioner, media/music/DJ, teaching assistant, hospitality/travel industry, youth worker.

Jonathan Ross

Jack of all trades (except anything practical), interested in finding fun and excitement in everything. An almost childlike sense of curiosity in everything that he finds interesting, but can become quickly bored. Imaginative, enthusiastic, sociable, friendly and adaptable. Do you share these qualities?

ENTP – Falcon

Falcons are the fastest animals in the world, flying up to about 190 kilometres (120 miles) per hour. ENTPs can also be fast with words and actions, moving quickly from idea to idea and task to task. Falcons migrate and ENTPs often like to try out new experiences. When they speak, falcons are loud and this is usually the case with ENTPs!

Strengths

Can enjoy variety and action.

Can communicate easily.

Enjoy learning new skills.

Are alert, outspoken and interesting company.

Can make decisions without being seen as soft.

Can be imaginative, spontaneous, problem solvers.

Can work on a number of things at once.

Are usually interested in the results/outcome.

As teenagers

They're adventurous, direct and assertive. They tend to ask why.

This can annoy others, who may think they're criticising them, but they're not: they're trying to understand why.

They can even be thought of as arrogant, but they're very critical, setting themselves high standards of performance.

They tend to be popular team members. Perhaps they should listen and be sensitive to others a bit more, and not criticise themselves, either.

As a boyfriend/girlfriend

They can be good fun to be with.

They try hard to impress their partner and they're usually witty and clever company.

They like to share their passions and beliefs.

They are very self-critical and can argue for their view with determination.

When they're pointing in a positive direction

They solve problems with imagination and enthusiasm.

They are confident, creative, honest, flexible,

They learn from mistakes, are fun to be with.

When they're pointing in a negative direction

They worry about their health, become quiet and sad.

They feel trapped.

To reduce stress?

Be kinder to yourself and others. Take a break and learn to recharge your batteries.

Your personality buzzwords

Imaginative, analytical and flexible.

Fame Academy

FAMOUS EXAMPLES (PROBABLY):

Peter Cook, Walt Disney, the Doctor (from *Doctor Who*), Q (from *Star Trek*), Tracy Beaker, Bob Geldof, Bugs Bunny, Lewis Carroll (author of *Alice in Wonderland*) and Billy Connolly – active imaginations focused on achieving their dreams.

Preferred learning style

They like group activity, discussion and role play.

They like to know the theory behind the idea.

They like logical order and to be able to show they understand the theory.

They like variety and choices.

Revision tips

Try to understand a subject fully before drawing your conclusions – little details are often important.

Stick to the point, prioritise and don't flit from idea to idea too quickly.

Preferred roles

Engineer, architect, inventor, creator, advocate, negotiator.

Job themes

Jobs in which they can solve problems creatively using their interest in theories and ideas, preferably with people around them.

IT (systems analyst, software designer), marketing, PR, management, science, engineering, journalism, architect, photographer, law, performer.

Degree-course ideas

Communication, media, journalism, performing arts (there are probably more stand-up comedians who are falcons than any of the other personalities), business, politics, law, philosophy, creative arts.

Job ideas that don't require loads of qualifications

Stonemason, engraver, props maker, toy maker/designer, picture framer, bingo caller, IT/website worker, tour guide, self-employment, retail, roadie, creative jobs.

Bob Geldof

In-your-face musician and campaigner. Will generally say what he believes is true even if it upsets some people. Uses determination, creativity and oral skills to seek out solutions to complex problems. An independent, flexible and analytical mind. Do you share these qualities?

ENTJ: Eagle

Eagles are symbols of power, leadership and strength. ENTJs can share these qualities, often soaring high to generate new ideas and new ways to do things. Others are often willing to follow ENTJs due to their good ideas and their determination to make them happen.

Strengths

Can enjoy action and variety.

Can focus on results and outcomes.

Can be imaginative, creative problem solvers.

Can take charge of situations and people easily.

Can follow plans and decide quickly.

Can make decisions without being seen as soft.

Can provide big ideas for better ways of doing things.

As teenagers

Often precocious (seem to be more mature than people of their age) and confident (which can be seen by some as big-headed, but it isn't: it's being able to stick up for what they believe in).

At their best they're strong, independent, intellectual and confident with high personal standards. They can be clever and respected leaders.

They might learn to be more tactful (consider others' feelings) and reflect more before plunging ahead!

As a boyfriend/girlfriend

They can be great fun to be with, though exhausting due to their drive and determination to lead and achieve things.

When they're pointing in a positive direction

They are good at analysing.

They stand up for what they believe in.

They are confident, creative, honest, get things done.

They learn from their mistakes, have fun.

When they're pointing in a negative direction

They become moody and unsure of their feelings.

To reduce stress?

You don't always have to be the leader. Listen to others now and again.

Your personality buzzwords

Determined, imaginative and achiever.

Fame Academy

FAMOUS EXAMPLES (PROBABLY):

Bill Gates, Richard Branson, Margaret Thatcher, Sherlock Holmes – natural leaders, through the strength of their beliefs!

Preferred learning style

They like group activity and discussion.

They like to know the theory behind the idea.

They like a clear order and a clear structure.

Revision tips

They're usually highly motivated to work on topics that interest them but they need to make sure they're thorough and get the simple things right.

Preferred roles

Inventor, entrepreneur, leader, architect.

Job themes

Managing people and/or resources in business or technical areas, e.g. catering/hospitality, travel, personnel, financial, public sector, retail management, operational/research analyst, journalism, politics, media work.

Self-employment.

Leading in the manufacturing, engineering and construction industries could also appeal.

Degree-course ideas

Business management, law, politics, history, computing/IT, environmental sciences, pure sciences.

Job ideas that don't require loads of qualifications

Market trader, ranger/warden, technician, van driver, painter and decorator, IT/website worker, window cleaner, politian, self-employment.

Richard Branson

One of the most famous and successful British entrepreneurs around. Sociable, visionary, objective and decisive. He is happy to learn from his mistakes, though his analytical mind ensures many a success. Has a go for it/let's-do-it attitude that spreads to those around him. Do you share these qualities?

Famous types*

ISTJ: Polar bear
Delia Smith
Alan Shearer
Michael Owen
Mark Darcy (from *Bridget Jones's Diary*)
Kelly Holmes

ISFJ: Koala bear
Mother Teresa
David Beckham
Piglet (from *Winnie-the-Pooh*)
Marge Simpson
Will Young

ISTP: Tiger
Clint Eastwood
Shrek
Tom Cruise
Ellen MacArthur

ISFP: Cat
Mozart
Rembrandt
Bill Oddie
Sir Paul McCartney
Ray Mears (explorer)

INFJ: Sea horse
Velma (from *Scooby Doo*)
Gandhi
Cinderella
Victoria Wood

INFP: Seal
William Shakespeare
Emily Brontë
Michael Palin
ET

INTP: Tawny owl
Albert Einstein
Charles Darwin
Isaac Newton
Caractacus Potts (from *Chitty Chitty Bang Bang*)
Tiger Woods

INTJ: Barn owl
Thomas Edison
Lisa Simpson
Mulder (from *The X Files*)
Morrissey
Willy Wonka
George Lucas

---

*Please remember that none of these people or characters have confirmed their preferences; this is a bit of fun, which allows us to explore type preferences in more detail!

ESTJ: Black bear
Victoria Beckham
Dr Gillian McKeith
Fred (from *Scooby-Doo*)
Rockefeller
Jordan/Katie Price

ESFJ: Teddy bear
Mary Poppins
Kylie Minogue
Dorothy (from *The Wizard of Oz*)
Gary Lineker
Daffy Duck

ESTP Panther
Madonna
Winston Churchill
Bart Simpson
Peter Pan
Tigger
James Bond
Liam Gallagher
Zorro

ESFP: Lion
Baloo (from *The Jungle Book*)
Shaggy and Scooby (from *Scooby-Doo*)
Donkey (from *Shrek*)
Bridget Jones
Freddie Flintoff
Ant and Dec
Charlotte Church

ENFJ: Dolphin
Martin Luther-King
Stephen Fry
Johnny Depp
Peter Kay
Rose Tyler (from *Doctor Who*)
Peter Ustinov

ENFP: Clown fish
Jamie Oliver
Paul O'Grady
Eamonn Holmes
The Little Mermaid
Terry Wogan
Anita Roddick

ENTP: Falcon
Billy Connolly
Walt Disney
Bob Geldof
Bugs Bunny
Peter Cook
Tracy Beaker
The Doctor* (from *Doctor Who*)

ENTJ: Eagle
Bill Gates
Margaret Thatcher
Richard Branson
Sherlock Holmes
Noel Gallagher

---

*The copy editor believes all the Doctors have different personalities. I believe they are all basically ENTP but show different amounts of the qualities associated with ENTP preferences. This reflects real life. There are millions of people with ENTP preferences, all are unique individuals united in similar signature strengths but expressed in different ways. What do you think reader?

My favourite Doctor was Tom Baker but I'm leaning more towards David Tennant now.

Learning and thinking better

'They know enough who know how to learn.'

Henry Adams

There are many different ways of describing how we learn. Here are four useful ways to explore learning styles.

Think of your potential to learn as being like a rubber band. It has a normal 'preferred' size when resting, as we have a normal preferred learning style, which is shown on this page.

First discover the ways we learn best. Our personality direction can help us choose learning places and methods that best suit us because we all learn best in different ways. Tick the boxes that match your preferences to discover your ideal ways to learn.

E	S	F	J	+
Learn best	**Learn best**	**Learn best**	**Learn best**	**Learn best**
Working in groups. When talking about the subject.	When they know why they are learning. When they know how they can use new learning.	With support and encouragement. When praised for good work.	When there is a clear structure and routine. With an accurate start and finish time.	When we're confident and relaxed. In the learning state.

I	N	T	P	-
Learn best	**Learn best**	**Learn best**	**Learn best**	**Learn best**
Somewhere quiet where they can concentrate without being interrupted.	When they know the theory behind the idea. When they can apply their learning in new ways.	When there is a logical order to follow. When they can demonstrate they can do or use the learning.	When there is a variety in the place and style of study.	When they learn from mistakes, and try again until they find a solution.

Once you know how you will learn best, why not speak to your learning provider about how they can support you with your learning?

A second way to think about learning styles is to be able to use all of the behaviours, or thinking styles, needed to solve problems. This is like stretching a rubber band, being able to change its shape to suit any situation faced.

Personality preferences are also a useful way to develop our full range of gathering all of the information we need to solve problems.

(Part Two of *The Buzz* describes ways in which we can develop the best of all ten.)

We can use these skills in the following ways:

E	I
Ask questions to help you fully understand the question or problem.	Listen carefully to all of the information and take it in. Research to make sure you collect enough information.
S	
Pay attention to the detail, the obstacles in the way. Look for the facts, the important information. Work through information in a step-by-step way. Ask what we can learn from the past.	**N**
	Step back from the detail and think about the problem in different ways. Ask, 'What could happen if we tried something completely different?' Focus on the solution or long-term aim and ask, 'If we were to achieve this, how would we think to get us there?'
T	**F**
Weigh up the options with pluses and minuses for each choice.	Consider the impact on people Ask, 'How are people involved?'
J	**P**
Plan your work so you will have enough time to complete it without a last-minute rush.	Stay alert to alternatives. Try different ways.
+	**-**
Enjoy yourself while working on the task; it is a challenge, so stay positive.	If you start to lose interest, go back and work through the approaches above to help you regain your enthusiasm.

Pictures, words and feelings

There's a third way to learn more. Many people now explore their preferred learning style within pictures, words or feelings.

Can you see what I mean?

We learn some things better as pictures – people's faces, maps and places.

- Describe the face of someone you know well (can you see it?).
- What's in your bedroom (can you see the walls, bed, clothes on the floor?)?

To develop your visual memory and skill take up drawing or painting, or redesign your bedroom (in your head).

That sounds good to me?

We learn some things best as words or sounds – songs and some number sequences.

- Jack and Jill went up the hill to … (the next words follow without your having to think).
- What's your telephone number?

To develop your hearing memory listen to songs, write and remember poems.

That feels right to me?

We learn some things best by the feelings we get, mostly in our stomach – called 'gut reaction' or 'instinct'. Physical skills – sports, dancing and driving – use this 'muscle memory'.

- Think of eating your favourite food, taste it now, mmm!
- Imagine lying in a lovely warm relaxing bath with bubbles all the way down to your toes.

To develop your 'muscle memory' take up a martial art, yoga, dancing or sport, or cook and eat what you make.

Are you a good speller?

Jonty is great at spelling. He pictures the word he's trying to spell, just in front of his forehead. Then he looks at each letter and checks whether it 'feels right'. If it does, he knows it's right; if not, he puts another letter there instead and checks the feeling again. This is how most good spellers do it (using seeing and feeling)!

A fourth way to enhance your learning is to enter the learning state, which has been shown to increase retention and recall.

On these next two pages, you can see not only how you behave in an argument, but also how other people you know are likely to argue!

In an argument, we tend to use our preferences. Tick the boxes that match yours. Is this how you argue?

E	S	F	J	+
Talk louder and faster ☐ Want to get things sorted out now! ☐	Argue specific facts ☐ Focus on details ☐	Personalise everything ☐ Sometimes just give in to keep the peace ☐	Jump to conclusions quickly ☐ Oversimplify issues ☐	Tend to sweep aside or ignore problems ☐

I	N	T	P	-
Would rather go away and think things through ☐ Keep quiet (until things build up so much that they explode!) ☐	Imagine huge consequences from small incidents ☐ Make sweeping generalisations ☐	Tell people not to 'get emotional' ☐ Say 'it's not personal' ☐	Throw in extra issues – 'and another thing' ☐ Argue both sides ☐	Imagine the worst is going to happen ☐ Pour cold water over any positive ideas, ☐ 'It'll never work!' ☐

How to get out of an argument!

Look at the ideas for each of your letters. They can help you get on better with other people.

E	S	F	J	+
Text or email ideas before springing them on people. Listen; talk only when the other person has finished.	Don't dismiss new ideas straightaway. Let others dream and fantasise.	Don't take everything personally. Don't be afraid of disagreement – sometimes it's healthy.	Consider all of the options before deciding. Remember – doing things the same way is not always the best.	Stay positive. Take seriously others' contributions and concerns; deal with them until an agreed way forward is found.

I	N	T	P	-
Allow people to talk through their ideas. Don't assume their ideas are rubbish because they're thinking out loud.	Don't ignore practical details. Consider how to get there – not just the finish line.	Consider people's emotions, not just the task and the goals. Say what's in it for people.	Focus on making decisions. Stick to the point.	Consider positive suggestions, not just the negatives. Agree an aim or solution all can work towards.

Choosing a course or career

We spend around 20 per cent of our waking lives at work, or 10 full years for 24 hours a day! So few decisions can be more important than, 'What course or career should I do?'

For most people, job satisfaction happens when we choose work that best matches our skills, behaviour, personality and identity. The following ideas are jobs that match personality preferences. They are intended to help us consider a wider range of courses and jobs than we might otherwise.

Don't think you should or should not consider a course or job because it isn't in the list alongside your preferences. Let the list help you explore your own personality as well as the jobs and courses.

Should I be an archaeologist?

One teenager said to me, 'I'm a tawny owl [INTP]. Should I be an archaeologist?'

Personality preferences alone cannot answer the question with a yes or no. Our preferences help us dig around and compare the tasks, training and prospects of a job with our own personality to help us come up with a really good match from the thousands of options available to us all.

It is a good idea to read through all of *The Buzz* before making a course or career decision.

Company culture – thinking inside the box?

Most bosses and even company cultures are probably ISTJ (polar bear) or ESTJ (black bear). How does this match with your preferences?

Companies often say they would like imaginative and creative people working for them (*N* preference). This is not usually the case at all! They generally prefer people who will follow the rules and procedures (*S* preference). So be careful. Someone recently told me she worked in a very *N* company – they had an 'imaginarium' – a room full of Lego, a blackboard and other stuff, in which people could go and be creative. Staff were encouraged to go in and their resulting ideas were valued. This is very unusual in organisations, but great for people with *N* preferences.

Happiest Job?

Can you guess in which job you find the happiest people?

Choose from rock stars, actors, footballers, teachers, hairdressers and TV presenters.

The answer is at the bottom of the next page.

Top ten employability skills

Employers ask for the same skills from staff. Which do you have? Half should be your natural preferences. Develop the others and you'll be in demand!

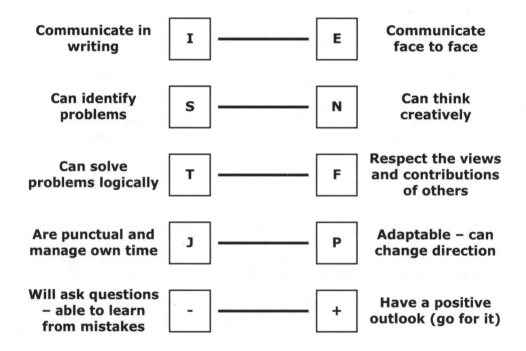

Communicate in writing	**I** ———— **E**	Communicate face to face
Can identify problems	**S** ———— **N**	Can think creatively
Can solve problems logically	**T** ———— **F**	Respect the views and contributions of others
Are punctual and manage own time	**J** ———— **P**	Adaptable – can change direction
Will ask questions – able to learn from mistakes	**-** ———— **+**	Have a positive outlook (go for it)

Interview tip:

Think of two examples that show you can use each of the above behaviours and an employer will be very impressed.

Answer to the question on the previous page: hairdressers. Did you guess correctly? In which job would you be happiest?

Type: strengths and stress

Preferences can help us recognise our strengths when faced with problems ...

Polar bear, koala bear, lion, panther	Barn owl, sea horse, falcon, clown fish	Tiger, tawny owl, black bear, eagle	Cat, seal, teddy bear, dolphin
Handle problems in a practical, realistic way. Use their experience to solve problems.	Approach problems with enthusiasm. See new possibilities.	Are good at analysing. Stand up for what they believe in.	Are good at describing the effect on people. Are good at making people feel included and valued.

But when we're stressed ...

Polar bear, koala bear	Barn owl, sea horse	Tiger, tawny owl	Cat, seal
Jump to the wrong conclusions. Imagine the worst is going to happen.	Overeat, drink too much or do too much exercise. Become easily annoyed and angry.	Have emotional outbursts and mood swings. Argue tiny details.	Criticise aggressively. Become obsessed with their 'right way'.

Panther, lion	Falcon, clown fish	Black bear, eagle	Teddy bear, dolphin
Have big ideas but don't know how to get there. Get confused about how they feel.	Worry about their health. Become sad and quiet. Feel trapped.	Become unsure of their feelings, especially towards other people. Have emotional outbursts and mood swings.	Take over without listening. Become martyrs, saying, 'Oh, I'll do it!' Dig their heels in.

71

Buying a present for someone?

Forget socks, slippers and smellies and try these ideas:

Polar bear, black bear

A small 'list' book so they can jot down their 'to do' list on the go.

Encourage them to make lists of things that make them feel good, too, not just lists of the stuff that needs to be done.

Tiger, cat

A day out to a favourite place, probably where there aren't a lot of other people about.

Panther

A day out somewhere fun and exciting, perhaps involving a challenge – perhaps a theme park or paintballing.

Lion

A day out somewhere fun and exciting, perhaps involving people – for example, a surprise party or gig.

Teddy bear

A surprise night out with all of their friends.

The latest mobile phone so they can text all of their friends and keep up with all of the gossip more often.

Koala bear, dolphin, sea horse

An album with photos of all the people they know with positive comments written by close friends and family.

Barn owl, eagle

A game, puzzle or challenge that is difficult to master, or the latest trendy gadget.

Seal, tawny owl

An 'ideas' book – somewhere to write down their good ideas as they happen. Challenge them to pick out the best ideas and share them with others.

Clown fish, falcon

An 'ideas' book – somewhere to jot down their good ideas as they occur. Challenge them to pick out the best and make them happen.

A surprise party, perhaps in fancy dress, where they are the centre of attention. Don't buy them something small: they'll just lose it!

How do you get on with your parents?

Take a look at their preferences (and yours on the opposite page). Try to understand them better and ask them to do the same for you.

Likely parenting style

Bears (polar, black, teddy, koala)

Tend to like setting rules and expect things to be done their way. Value traditions, family roles and explaining right and wrong through 'should', 'dos' and 'don'ts'. Tend to remove 'treats' as punishment.

Cats (tiger, panther, cat, lion)

Tend to be hands-off in approach, encouraging their children to explore, spread their wings and learn by doing. They are hard to fool. Tend to become strict if disobeyed.

Sea animals (clown fish, dolphin, sea horse, seal)

Tend to be encouraging, like everyone to get on well, take care of and support each other. Can try to impose their own 'hippie' values on those close to them. Tend to withdraw love and support as punishment.

Birds (tawny owl, barn owl, eagle, falcon)

Tend to encourage children to develop a wide range of skills. May enjoy discussion and playing games/quizzes with their children. Tend to remove 'privileges' as punishment.

Note: Parent/child can be substituted for members of other relationships, such as friendships, marriages and working relationships.

Likely child style

Bears

Tend to like to know what the rules are and be shown how to do things. Generally, like to help. Value safety and respond well to praise when completing task 'properly'.

Cats

Tend to be bold and daring and interested in physical activities (music, art, sports, events, holidays, socialising) and like having fun.

Sea animals

Are deep and inventive, think through their feelings, are sensitive. Respond well to imagination and helping others. Can get lost in the world of their ideas.

Birds

Are imaginative and curious, don't like being told what to do without a logical reason. Can seem to argue, but they need to ask why and have answers. Can be very self-critical.

Remember, we're all OK. Just different!

Section Two

Make Your Behaviour Buzz

Section Two
Make Your Behaviour Buzz

We make better decisions when we're in better moods. Positive mood mostly equals positive decision.

Milk rage

I recently saw someone at work in the kitchen trying to open a carton of UHT skimmed milk with a blunt knife (the sort of knife that only just cuts through mashed potato – certainly not the card the carton of milk is made of, which could probably survive a journey to Jupiter). She was in a very negative mood, combining frustration, anger and desperation. In that mood the only thing she was likely to cut was herself.

I took the carton of milk from the woman, went and found a pair of scissors and then cut the carton calmly and carefully. Good result, milk in our coffee and not all over the bench and our clothes; no visit to A&E!

The same thing happens to people all the time. They wait until they are angry, sad or desperate before making decisions. It is hardly surprising that their decisions are as poor as their mood.

To control our behaviour, we need to notice how we do moods. Over the next few pages, I'd like you to check out how you 'do' some moods – relaxed, angry, bored, go for it, nervous and curious, happy and sad.

We tend to do them in very similar ways.

Think about where the feeling starts in your body, the direction it moves (up, down, around), how hot or cold it is and the speed of the feeling. Do you feel them the way they're described?

Angry

This mood is bad. How do you do it? Try it here only so you know why it's worth avoiding it for ever!

Think about someone (or something) that makes you angry now. See the face of the person who makes you angry so closely that you can smell their stinky breath and feel as if they were getting under your skin now.

Do you experience anger as a feeling that moves quickly up the body, feels hot and uncomfortable? Most people do.

That's why people say, 'I've had it up to here with you!' pointing to their head, because anger gets trapped there. That's why people go red when angry. Anger feels bad and makes us feel as if we're not in control. This is why anger is bad for our health and that of those around us. It usually explodes out of our mouths or fists.

Anger is like a fizzy-drink bottle that has been violently shaken. The pressure builds inside with nowhere to go until the top is released and you get sprayed in fizzy wet drink.

Tip: Try releasing the top of a shaken fizzy drink. Do it *slowly*, so the pressure is released gently. Imagine the same when you're angry. Think of your body as the shaken bottle and imagine releasing it slowly from your body. This way no one gets covered in anger – or fizzy drink!

Oh, and don't try this on your parents' new settee or you might see how they do anger!

Relaxed

Think about a time you felt really relaxed. Go back to the time and place now – see what you saw, hear what you heard and feel what you felt.

Notice the direction, speed and temperature of the feelings in your body.

Most people say being relaxed feels nice and moves slowly and gently down their bodies like cool or warm waves.

Use this sensation whenever you need to feel relaxed and calm:

- after exercise;
- to wind down before going to bed;
- to calm down after a stressful experience;
- any time you want to give your body a boost.

Bored

Think of a time you were really bored. Remember it now, where you were and what it felt like. Boredom is an uncomfortable place to be. It is usually a flat, heavy, prickly, tingly and slow feeling – a constipated, not complicated, feeling.

We also feel slightly 'out of it' and 'not quite there'. Our attention wanders off.

This is an awful mood to be in when we're learning. We don't remember much when bored.

It is important for teachers and students to avoid this mood in learning situations. Making topics interesting or allowing students to move about helps avoid boredom.

Young children are naturally great learners because they don't 'do bored' (until they've learned it at school). They look for something interesting in every situation, or move on to something else until they find something interesting. We could all benefit from unlearning how to be bored! A walk in the rain can become interesting when a child sees a wriggling worm or lady-bird for the first time.

Now you know what being bored is – stay away from it!

Go for it or buzzing

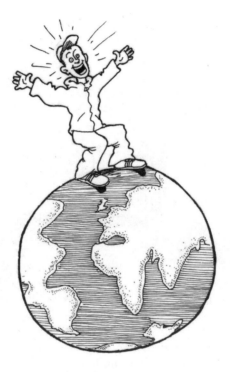

This is an on-top-of-the-world feeling, a time we feel we can achieve what we desire and are in complete control.

To access it, think about a time you felt really good. Step back into the time and place – see what you saw, hear what you heard and feel what you felt.

Notice the direction, speed and temperature of the feeling in your body. It tends to go up the centre of the body and brings calm confidence. It's as if the feeling comes out where it's needed: the mouth for singing or presenting, the foot for playing football, and so on.

Spin the feeling so it comes back into your body and goes round and round, making you feel better each time.

Nervous

Nervousness is a popular but unhelpful mood. It is a spiky, tingly feeling that for most people starts in their stomach and spreads out, filling the body with nasty butterflies and turning their voices squeaky and their legs to jelly.

We usually use this feeling to perform badly at things!

There is a lack of control and butterflies in our stomach. So don't use this one! Turn this into 'curious' or 'go for it' and better results usually follow.

To access this feeling, think of an exam or interview you've had that went badly and you'll not be far from the feeling. *Urghh!*

Many teenagers spend a lot of their time in this mood. *Don't.* Try out a go for it, 'relaxed' or 'curious' mood instead – and stay there.

Curious

This mood has an 'ooh' sound! It is when we feel drawn in, pulled towards something that will be good and nice.

It's sort of a nice tingly feeling – the opposite of nervousness in feeling.

Different bits of us can feel pulled towards the object of the mood: our heart if it's curious about an attractive person, our stomach if it's lovely food or our head if it's an idea we're attracted to. Think of something that really interests you and you'll find curiosity.

This is a fantastic mood to use more of the time. If you're curious while you're with a person, you'll be more interested and attentive – and they'll usually be more interested in you! If you're curious during learning, you'll remember more!

Sad

Sadness is a sinking, cool feeling. It is usually heavy, flat and uncomfortable.

It is similar to boredom, but feels worse because it is a stronger pull, usually through the middle of our body. Some people describe it as feeling like a toilet being flushed, leaving their body sort of empty and hurting.

A mood best avoided.

Think about entering a positive mood instead. Can you think about a positive outcome to the situation that makes you too sad? If not, the 'energy bubble' technique (see Page 117) can protect you from this mood.

Happy

Happiness is a mood that is usually light, warm, moves up and out, and tingles nicely. It often starts in the heart area and is a solid and content feeling.

This is a great 'background' mood to be in. To try it, think of things that make you happy.

Songs, people, memories of holidays and nights out, favourite TV characters and so on. Then bus journeys can be 'happy' rather than 'boring'.

I am sure you noticed that each pair of moods you've explored are opposite – one bad, one good:

(–) **angry** – **relaxed** (+)

(–) **bored** – **go for it** (+)

(–) **nervous** – **curious** (+)

(–) **sad** – **happy** (+)

We feel good when experiencing positive moods and bad when in negative moods.

We can choose which mood to be in. Can you guess which moods are the most useful?

It's OK to feel the negative emotions now and again but some people stay in them for their whole lives! What a waste!

Be a mind-reader

Play this game to read someone's mind and learn more about moods.

Ask the person to think of a place or someone who can make them feel either angry or happy, or any from the moods you've just learned. Anger and happiness are usually easy to 'read'. Ask them to stand up (it's easier to spot), close their eyes and pretend they are with this person and to feel the speed, direction and temperature of the feeling as it fills their whole body. As you encourage them, notice how they move, especially in their face. Are their muscles tense or relaxing? Are they clenching their teeth (angry) or smiling (happy) or dropping their jaw (relaxed)? Ask them to keep thinking of the person, perhaps something they say, until you have read their mind! With a bit of practice you'll be able to read all eight moods described above.

Five steps to mood control

- Think of the mood you need (relaxed, go for it, happy).
- Picture a time you were strongly and fully in this mood. Make it big, bold and bright; step into it.
- Add some suitable music, perhaps a song you know well and the sounds you heard. Blast it out big and bold.

- Now feel the feeling and double it, and double it again.
- Capture it with an anchor (see 'Anchors' below) and use your mood when you need it.

Anchors

Choose from this list or make up new ones:

- Press your thumb and a finger together.
- Press your tongue up into the roof of your mouth.
- Curl up your toes on one foot or both.
- Take a deep breath in and out (we do this naturally for courage).
- Touch a part of your body, such as your knee, wrist or forearm.

You need to perform your chosen anchor when you're holding in your mind a mood you really like, so that your brain associates the mood with the gesture – the anchor.

You can test whether it works by setting off the anchor later. If it works, and brings back the mood you want, great; if not, run though the sequence again until it works – it really is worth the bother!

You can set off all sorts of anchors. I have a friend who has anchored feeling confident, in control and friendly to the act of shaking hands with someone – every time. This sounded such a good one that I've borrowed it! It *is* good.

A woman told me she was making her two-year-old nephew laugh and touched her nose while doing it. Later, she touched her nose again and her nephew laughed again.

Benefits of mood control

Research links many benefits to positive moods:

- less stress;
- better health;
- making better choices;
- more happiness;

- more friends;
- better performance (in exams, interviews, presentations);
- removal of anger and conflict.

Mood can be spread from person to person. Spread positive moods and, as a side effect, your charisma will increase!

Anchoring to control anger

Jason was in trouble at school. He had lost his temper a number of times, had fights, threatened staff. He was taught how to avoid becoming angry by anchoring a calm, relaxing feeling. Instead of being excluded from school, Jason is now in control of his mood and is much happier.

'I can hardly believe it works,' he said. 'I feel in control of my own body now. Family, friends and teachers now know they can talk to me and I can stay chilled.'

Mood control

Sometimes we decide to be in a particular mood. You may be the first to arrive in an empty classroom and start thinking about the dull lesson ahead and feel bored. Then a person you really fancy walks in and you quickly decide to be in a different mood – happy and excited (or nervous). Hearing post drop through the letterbox and hearing a telephone or mobile phone seems to snap most of us into a curious mood the instant we hear the ring.

Mostly, we change moods without thinking about it. One of the most important things you can learn in life is that you can control your mood! And it's not even very hard to do. You just need to think of the mood you'd like to be in, the mood most likely to get you the result you desire.

Then think about a time you were in that mood. Remember it in vivid detail, see what you saw, the colours, shapes, people and/or objects. Hear the sounds and let the feeling overwhelm you. Imagine you're sitting watching yourself on a huge cinema screen having this positive feeling, then step into the picture, sounds and feeling fully.

Then capture the feeling by anchoring it. Choose different anchors for different moods.

You drive me mad!

Some people let other people control their moods. This is really daft! They say things, such as:

- 'You make me so angry.'
- 'You drive me mad.'

There are times when this can be OK. Some people, TV programmes and songs can take us to positive moods, such as 'in love', 'happy' and 'excited'.

But it is generally best to be in control of your own moods, especially when you are around 'mood hoovers'.

Research links many problems to bad moods: sleep problems, skin complaints, asthma, colds and flu, being tired and run down, headaches and digestive troubles and even more serious illnesses have been linked to remaining in bad moods. Perhaps they are our body's way of asking us to move in a positive direction.

A negative direction: mood hoovers!

Have you noticed how some people are miserable? Most of the time they tend to have a frown on their face. When these people head our way, we think, 'Oh no, not him (or her)!' and we hope they didn't see us because we know that, as soon as they start talking, they'll make us feel as miserable as they are.

I used to work with a really miserable woman. On my way to my office, I'd pass a kitchen and, if she was in it, I'd tiptoe quietly past, hoping she wouldn't hear me. If she did, she would start talking and it felt as if she were sucking out all of my life force and energy. If she'd won the Lotto, she'd still be miserable: she'd whine, 'Well it wasn't a Rollover, I only won three million.' They leave us feeling hoovered empty, like a squeezed-out lemon skin.

These people talk in a voice like fingernails scraping their way down a blackboard or the Child Catcher from *Chitty Chitty Bang Bang*. They love saying things like, 'I told you so': 'That's ruined my day, that has'; 'I hate Mondays'; 'I can't wait until I retire!'

We can all feel negative sometimes but some people stay there their whole life. What a hole to be in! Pity. Research suggests these people have poorer health, fewer friends and less happiness and success than those of us who aim in a positive direction.

Mood hoovers try to stamp on our dreams. Worse, they stamp on their own dreams.

A positive direction: mood movers and groovers!

Other people seem to be happier, brighter and more cheerful. When they enter the room you're in, you think, 'Great, they're fun!' and you smile inside, feeling good. These are great people to be around because moods spread, and we're kind of drawn towards them naturally, probably because these people tend to be happier and more successful and some of it rubs off on us and inside of us. This is the basis of charisma. If you want more charisma, move in a positive direction.

I worked with someone who had a great effect on those he worked with. He was able to laugh at himself and make us feel good about ourselves. He had a bad back – enough to make some people very miserable – but he made the best of it because he thought life was too short. He once had to go for a CAT scan (a whole-body X-ray). The next day, we asked him how he got on. He told us he'd found the room OK. The nurse told him to go behind the screen, take off his clothes and put on the gown.

'I went behind the screen, took off all my clothes and put on the gown,' he told us. 'I noticed the gown only came down to just below my bellybutton. I thought, "Oh, this doesn't cover my modesty." Then I thought, "Oh, well, they're medical people: they know what they're doing." So I walked out from behind the screen. The nurse then looked at me and said, "Aren't you going to put on the trousers?" I went behind the screen, where the trousers had fallen behind a chair.'

Another time, he was at an important meeting and thought everyone was staring at him. When he went to the toilet and saw himself in the mirror, he realised the pen he had been chewing had leaked blue ink all over his mouth. It looked awful. It looked worse after he tried to scrub it off and left a big red mark around the blue one.

Laughter: the shortest distance between two people

This colleague was happy to share all of his experiences and enjoy them with us. Life is about having experiences and not being so boring that we do nothing for fear of looking silly. Don't worry: if you do, people will identify with you and laugh *with* you. They laugh at *us* only when we try to cover things up, lying to others or ourselves.

Smile. It may happen. Victor Borge said laughter is the shortest distance between two people. Laughing is also the quickest way to get from negative to positive, from hoover to groover. A smile not only lights up your own face, inside and out, but also delights those around us. Wow, what a bonus!

Hoovers say, 'I'll laugh about this in ten years' time.'

Groovers say, 'I'll laugh about it now and avoid wasting ten whole years of my life.'

Moving in a positive direction

If a positive direction and positive moods are so good, why would anyone ever point in a negative direction?

One answer comes from the way we learn. To learn, we need to try, have a go and be prepared not to master every skill first time round. David Beckham probably didn't get his first-ever free kick in the top corner of the net. He didn't give up, but practised and practised. Most things we learn take lot of practice – learning to talk, walk, tie our shoelaces, read, write, catch a ball, drive, fly a plane are all big achievements.

When a baby first starts to make gurgling word sounds, we offer encouragement, not criticism. We don't shout at them to stop. We don't yell, 'Shut up! Speak properly! It's a *cup*, a cup! Not a phut-phut! You stupid baby! You can't talk! You're a disgrace to yourself and your family! Crawl to your room – *now*!'

That would be silly, going in a negative direction, but that's what most children and adults get used to as they get older.

Sea squirts

Researchers have found that for every positive comment a parent makes to their children, they make nine negative comments. Parents are surprised, because they think the balance is around half and half. Parents, teachers and friends don't mean to be so mean. Smile as you encounter negative comments; use the bubble technique (see 'Energy bubble' on Page 117) to make them bounce off you. Years of hearing that we're not good enough can be enough to ensure we stay that way throughout our whole lives.

Sea squirts are interesting animals. As babies they swim along the ocean floor until they find a rock. Then they latch on to it and stay there for the rest of their lives. Once stuck on a rock, they eat their own brains, because they don't need one any more – they've settled somewhere. They are also called dead man's fingers. Some people behave in the same way: they settle in a negative place, using negative behaviour and getting negative results. Some people stay there for years. Some form bands and sing about it. If someone sings to you, 'I feel like a cat in a bag waiting to drown' or 'Why does it always rain on me?' reply, 'Because you're pointing in a negative direction, mate!'

Do we wheelie do this?

People stay in a negative direction and in a negative place because they are scared they'll make a mistake and look stupid if they try something new; so they stick with what they know, even if that is very negative. A man I knew has to take his wheelie bin down a bit of a steep hill to get it on the pavement for the refuse collectors. One cold winter's day it slipped from beneath him as he was pushing it down the hill. It was full and smacked into the path at the bottom of the hill. His nose smacked into the plastic bar along the top of the bin. Although it really hurt, he said the first thing he did was look around to make sure no one had seen him. We all do this sort of thing, scared to look silly, to look as if we've made a mistake. People often run for a bus and miss it, then, instead of stopping, they slow down gradually, so they don't look silly.

Once we stop playing such a silly game, learn what learning is really about, we can be happier, healthier and learn far more skills and have far more fun.

If you occasionally find yourself turning in a negative direction, just move back to front and into a positive direction: from 'angry' to 'relaxed', from 'bored' to 'go for it', from 'stressed' to 'laughing'. Imagine a huge compass inside your heart or head that quickly points you back in the right direction.

A stinky but

What keeps many people in a negative direction is a stinky 'but':

- ... *but* I'm not clever (or I'm overqualified);
- ... *but* I'm too old (or too young);
- ... *but* I'm not very attractive.

Stinky buts can be cleaned up. If my children reveal a stinky 'but' I threaten to put them in the shower to clean up their bad language. Our shower is broken and the water icy cold, so they change direction quickly.

There are too many people who are not really clever, not very attractive, too old and too young who are successful, happy and confident. When you notice you have a stinky but, you can clean it up now.

Darren's story

Darren contacted me recently to tell me how he was doing.

His letter is inspirational. I saw Darren three years ago. He'd left school at sixteen with no qualifications and started working in a place that recycled pallets. He'd thought he'd work there for only about a year because the work was hard, the pay low, the conditions a bit dangerous and his boss grumpy.

He came to see me, a careers adviser, when he was twenty-nine, still in the same job, thirteen years later.

Why had he stayed in the job for so long?

'I was going to leave – but I'm not that clever.'

He had two other stinky buts – three on one person is quite smelly! Darren had waited thirteen years; some wait longer.

'What do you want to get from this meeting?' I asked him.

'Well, there's a school reunion next year and I have to be training to be a physiotherapist by then,' he said, looking determined. A positive direction with a goal on the end can be a great thing.

After a short chat, we worked out that he wanted to be a sports therapist in a football club. He wrote to me telling me what had happened since:

> The school reunion was great. I had started on the sports therapy course and was really enjoying it. Even better, I'm now working at a Premiership football club and can hardly believe it. I remember your story about your first day at work and think I've bettered it.

I'd told Darren a story about a really embarrassing first day at work I'd had, in order to encourage him to start something new and keep going despite any setbacks on the way.

He certainly had a more embarrassing first day than mine. He'd accidentally jumped the lunch queue, because he was so nervous, ahead of millions of pounds' worth of players who should have gone first (club rules). He went on to say how this turned out really well because the players all knew who he was, and it broke the ice. Bad stuff can be good, depending on how we use it.

Try this out

Here are two ways you can experience the power of a positive direction.

1. Next time you do something a bit silly, you can either hide it or tell someone about it. Choose someone to share your story with and notice the reaction. They'll often tell you something similar that happened to them. They'll usually smile and you'll both feel better.
2. Give deserved praise. Next time someone does something well, let them know. Or tell a friend something you really like about them (such as friendliness, humour or something from the 'Personality buzzwords' list on Page 4). Notice their response. You are pointing them in a positive direction. They'll glow and grow.

57 channels and there's nothing on

Watching TV can be a great way to be pulled in a negative direction.

Warning: Watching the news can seriously damage your health. It seems to be designed to drag us into a negative place. Wherever in the world bad stuff is happening, they'll take us there with horrific pictures of death, pain, anger, misery – *urghh!* If it bleeds it leads. There seems to be little or no place for good news, even when the news goes on and on for 24 hours.

So many programmes seem to rely on our watching people argue with each other.

Magazines tell us we're not good enough as we are, we need to be better dressed, more attractive, fitter, richer, or have more of this or that to be as happy as the celebrities who infect our TV screens and magazines. It's all a myth, a mistake, designed to make us buy stuff. A guaranteed way not to be happy and confident is to buy all that rubbish.

The bottom line

The cure? Concentrate on being the best you can be. Not a copy of someone else. Each year, thousands of teenagers are now going through the agony of cosmetic surgery to change the shape of their noses, ears, waists, bottoms and so on. Most just want to look a bit more like someone else. The sad thing is, they don't realise that, when someone falls in love with you, they fall in love with *you as you are*, with your eyes, ears, feet and bottom *as they are now*.

If someone says to you, 'I'll love you only if your bottom looks more like Kylie's or Robbie's,' then there is something wrong with them, not you or your bottom. I'm glad we got to the bottom of that because finding out our strengths, discovering ways we can use them and then going for it is what life is all about, and a great time to start is now.

Finding our natural mood

Flexibility of behaviour is very useful. You choose your mood to ensure you can return unwanted goods. Choose the mood that will bring you the behaviour you need for each situation you face and you will be a happier and more successful person.

Complete the following sentence:

My life is like _____

Because _____

_____

The 'because' gives clues as to which is your natural mood, the one you're in the majority of the time.

Is your life like a roller-coaster full of excitement and adventure? Is it like a battle against people who're trying to get you down?

Guess which is healthier.

If you'd like to have a great background mood, try one of the *positive* moods from Section 2.

It seems we all have a natural mood. When your natural mood is good you are good. This is when you'll know you're sorted.

Research into happiness shows that, one year after winning millions on the Lotto, people return to the same level of happiness as before their win. If you were a miserable sod before winning the lottery you are likely to be a miserable sod one year after winning it. If you were a happy person before, you'll be a happy person after. Similar effects are described when couples have a baby in order to feel happier, but it is after two years that they return to their original levels of happiness. Shopping sprees generally give a very short burst of happiness. The techniques in *The Buzz* show us how to create long-term happiness for ourselves.

Remember that all moods are useful in some situations but not in others: disgust is useful to stop you eating when you're full but not so useful when you've been asked to taste a meal someone has made for you.

All you need to do is choose the right mood for the situation – if this sounds simple it's because it is.

'In life pain is inevitable but suffering is optional.'

Hedy Schleifer

Do you need to ask for directions?

On a sunny day, a wise student, Cathy, was sitting by the entrance about to eat her packed lunch. A new student approached her and asked if this was Roker Park College. She nodded. 'Are the students of this college friendly?' he asked. Cathy replied by saying, 'Tell me first about the students from where you come from.'

'They're very friendly, kind, warm, buzzing people,' he said. Cathy said, 'Then I'm pleased to inform you that the students from this college will be the same.' The new student smiled, thanked Cathy and went on his way, head high and excited.

Before Cathy could start her lunch, another student approached her and asked the same question as the first. She nodded again. 'Are the students of this college friendly?' he asked. Cathy replied by saying, 'Tell me first about the students from where you come from.'

Cathy could tell from the badge on his sports bag that this student came from the same place as the first. He said, 'They're mean, sad, angry people, down, flat and cold.' Cathy replied, 'Then I'm afraid to have to tell you that the people of this college will be the same.' The student, shoulders down, wearily walked on into the college.

I can canoe, can you?

Anne was finally offered a place on a training course she wanted to do. Then she was told she would have to go on an outdoor trip, which included jumping in a lake at the start of the course and before canoeing. She can't swim well and, even though she'd be wearing a life jacket and the water would be only waist high, she said she wasn't going. With the help of an adviser, she anchored a feeling of confidence to the moment she jumped in the water.

She went on the trip and said as she jumped in the lake that she felt great! 'I'm so glad I did it. I've made some great new friends, though they took the mickey out of me for not being able to swim well. I'll use anchoring confidence to help me do more things now.'

In which direction do you face?

These teenagers show us how it's done!

Be your worst – *urghh!*

Peter never returns stuff he buys that he doesn't like. 'I imagine the shop assistant and people in the queue staring at me and thinking I'm tight, and I feel nervous butterflies in my stomach. I say to myself, "Oh, I'll just keep it," to stop myself feeling so nervous.'

Amy is a good swimmer but she bottles it at important events. 'I make myself nervous before a race by thinking about how bad I'd feel if I mess it up. I look at other swimmers and think they look better than me. A voice says, "You're going to be last." Sometimes I get so nervous it drains my energy and I just want the race to be over.'

John is a good 100-metres runner for the county. He is not good at talking to girls he fancies. 'I imagine them saying, "You're ugly" or "You're stupid to think I'd fancy you".

'Then I picture me standing next to the girl, looking embarrassed and stupid. Then I get nervous and I don't talk to the girl. I feel better for a while but then I'm annoyed with myself for being a coward.'

John is proof that we all use bad thinking in some parts of our lives and good thinking in other parts of our lives. It's not we who are hopeless: it's just our thinking in this one part of our life.

The trick is to change the bad thinking to good thinking, as we see on the next page.

Thinking for failure

1. Say, 'I can't' or 'I'll fail' or 'I'll not bother'.
2. Picture a negative outcome, the worst that could happen (as a movie scene or photograph).
3. Feel nervous or stressed out or stupid. Feel it intensely! *Urghh!* Repeat Steps 1–3 until you're ready to fail or walk away from the activity

In which direction do you face?

These teenagers show us how it's done!

Be your best – *mmm!*

Suzanne is good at returning the clothes she buys then decides she doesn't want. She says to herself, 'I'll take this back – I can get my money back.' Then she imagines the money in her hand or the lovely things she can buy with it. This makes her feel good and buzzing. She then enjoys going back to the shop.

John is the runner we met earlier. Before a race, he looks at each opponent, spots a potential weakness, and says, in his head, 'I can beat you.' Just before he runs, he says, 'I'm going to run the best I can.' He imagines how good it will feel to win the race. He builds the feeling up and up to a peak (buzzing) before the start of the race. Then he runs.

Nicola is good at talking to lads she fancies. She says, 'I'm going to talk to him. If he likes me, fine; if not, there are plenty more shoes in the shop!' She then imagines they're both talking and getting on well together. This makes her feel buzzing! The words, the pictures and feelings give Nicola the confidence and motivation to talk to the lads she fancies.

If they don't like her, she's fine about it because of her shoes-in-the-shop way of framing the experience.

Note: This thinking does not mean everyone will fancy you, but it does give you your best chance of impressing someone by being at your best.

Thinking for success

1. Say, 'I can', 'I can do it', 'I can win' and 'I'll do my best'.
2. Picture a positive outcome, the result you desire (as a movie scene or photograph). Intensify the sights and sounds.
3. Feel buzzing or go for it. Enjoy feeling it intensely. Repeat Steps 1–3 until you're ready to go! *Mmm!*

Catchphrases as a way to influence our mood

Ever been relaxed and then realised you're late? Suddenly you go from being relaxed to panic! Ever been in a bad mood and then someone you fancy has walked into the room and suddenly you smile and your mood is positive? Moods can change quickly. Staying in very good ones is the one very good thing you can do.

Moods can be useful to help us create better futures as well as presents. Affirmations or catchphrases are used by top performers to achieve their best. We can all use them. They build powerful moods and encourage positive behaviour.

What do you repeat to yourself? Whether it's negative (e.g. 'I'll never be happy') or positive, the chances are you'll become your thoughts. So choose positive catchphrases. Write them down – it makes them more real. Successful people do.

Our catchphrases should:

- start with 'I';
- be in the present tense;
- be a positive achievement.

1. You can start by thinking of a problem: 'I don't like new situations.'
2. Then the mood you enter from this: 'I feel nervous and scared.'
3. Then think of the solution: 'I like new situations.'
4. The mood you enter from this solution: 'I feel confident and learn new things!'
5. Then turn it into a catchphrase: 'I like new situations; I feel confident and learn new things.'

Now think of a problem you'd like to overcome.

Problem: _____

Negative mood: _____

Solution: _____

Positive mood: _____

Catchphrase: _____

Life is not a game of cards

So far we've explored five chunks of personality and discovered our natural strengths and behaviour. Then we looked at how we do moods, so we can start to take control of our behaviour.

Next we can learn how to use the best of all ten for fully flexible behaviour.

Some people say life is like a game of cards: we're dealt a hand (our personality preferences) and it's then up to us how we play it (our behaviour and moods). I disagree. If the hand we're dealt is not useful for a challenge we face, it is better to go back to the pack and pick out the best cards for the game or challenge. My son learned to do this when he was just four! With *The Buzz*, we can have all ten behaviours and pick out whichever positive mood is most useful for the challenge in front of us. When I saw my son doing this with cards, he'd say, 'It's not cheating: it's winning!' I encourage him to do the same in life by using all ten of the following:

E	I
Being aware of people and things around us	Being aware of our own bodies and feelings
N	**S**
Being focused on the future and possibilities	Being focused on the present and reality
F	**T**
Being totally involved in the experience	Being able to step back and observe
P	**J**
Being flexible	Being decisive
-	**+**
Facing in a negative direction	Facing in a positive direction

The best of *E*

There are times when we need to influence people around us. We may need to persuade, convince, entertain, inform, educate or train. To do this well we need confidence. This is when we need to point in the *E+* direction.

E+ is like being a perfect host/hostess. This is about being aware of people and things outside of our body. Focus on the people you are talking to, not yourself. Concentrate on making sure they have a good time and you're using the best of E behaviour.

Two techniques you can use that further develop your *E+* are 'walking tall' and 'chocolate voice'.

Walking tall

Stand with the back of your head, your shoulders, your bum and your heels touching a flat wall, looking straight ahead (and slightly down). Practise walking in this position. You'll look and feel more confident. It may feel a bit odd at first but keep going: it really does make a difference! It is a great way to walk into a room looking confident and determined, perhaps in an interview. A TV programme recently claimed part of the success of the band Oasis is due to Liam Gallagher's rock-star walk!

Chocolate voice

Our voice is the main way we interact with the world around us. We all have two natural voices. We have a squeaky, higher-pitched voice that seems to come from our throat or nose, which projects lies, nerves or lack of confidence. We also have a deeper, calmer voice that seems to start in our stomach and projects confidence, assurance, authority and wisdom. Which voice do you think is the more useful?

To develop your chocolate voice, first imagine the taste of chocolate in your mouth (or something else nice if you don't like chocolate). Then take a deep breath, hold it for a second, then breathe out slowly and calmly from your stomach and make an 'mmmm' sound as you taste the chocolate. When you're doing it well you'll notice a vibrating quality to the sound that makes you feel good.

Use your chocolate voice when you need to be confident and you'll notice people taking more notice of you!

Guess which of these people were voted Best Voice by a group of 80 teenagers I was working with last year: Davina McCall, Jade Goody (*Big Brother*), George Clooney and David Beckham.

Answer: the first man and woman named were voted Best Voice.

Chocoholic?

Chocolate makes us feel good because it encourages the release of serotonin in the brain – a chemical that makes us feel good. Research has shown that we can increase the release of serotonin just by thinking of happy memories! Try it now. Mmm. Ooh! The reverse is also true. Thinking of bad things can make us ill. Remember: chewing tin foil or swallowing chocolate. It is your choice.

The best of *I*

There are times when we need to be aware of our own body and its needs – to balance the needs of relaxation, food, drink, exercise and sleep.

Sometimes, clocks, deadlines and work can shift our focus on tasks and take our attention away from ourselves. At times this is good; at other times it is bad. Balancing requires us to develop the best of *E* and *I*. You can be a 100 per cent 'party animal' some of the time and a totally cool, laid-back, chilled-out dude at other times. Doing both full on is better than muddling them up, like people who say they're relaxed when they are hyper!

When we hear people say things such as, 'I'm happy in myself' and 'That coat is just not me', it is a sign they are using *I*: they are making decisions by checking out how they feel inside first. Here are three games you can use to boost your *I*+: 'Really relaxing', 'Inner voice', 'Identity parade'.

'Really relaxing'

Think of the activities you do that make you feel really relaxed. List them. Having a long bath, listening to your favourite music, sport, walking the dog, sunbathing are some of the favourites. (Watching TV doesn't count because it is a passive activity, a sort of neutral activity that generally passes time – unless you watch horrible stuff such as the news or programmes that deal with holidays/DIY/builders/takeaways from Hell, because you're probably going to feel bad after watching these. The exceptions to this rule are watching TV with friends or family, talking about it and enjoying it as an occasion or watching stuff that makes you really laugh – these are good for us.)

How often do you spend doing these? Can you do more of them? While you're doing them, be aware that you're relaxing, enjoy yourself and don't feel guilty or start worrying about other stuff. Just enjoy the activity itself. Be pleased that you've found the time and place to relax to boost your immune system (it fights disease) and release endorphins (more of our body's natural feel-good chemicals). Research confirms that just twenty minutes per day can have amazingly positive health effects.

'Inner voice'

'I knew at the time I shouldn't have done it,' is something we hear from other people or ourselves. We often know more than we are consciously aware of.

To prove this, try the following game:

1. Think of a decision you need to make. Phrase it as a problem with a yes/no answer, or, 'Should I do x or should I do y?'

2. Now clear your head, relax and run through the question with one of the answers. As you imagine the outcome, be aware of how you feel, what you see, hear, smell etc. Notice how you feel across your body.

3. Now clear your head, relax and run through the question with the other one of the answers. As you imagine the second answer, be aware of how you feel, what you see, hear, smell. Notice how you feel across your body.

4. Now which was better? First or second? If one was better, you have your answer! If neither was better, you need to rephrase the question and repeat the exercise.

This approach to decision making has been used for hundreds of years. One version is placing a black (for yes) and a white (for no) stone in your pocket when you face a dilemma. You then choose a stone without knowing which decision to make. Your reaction when you see the stone will tell you if it is the right or wrong decision. You normally instinctively feel, 'I'm pleased it's that stone' or 'I wish it were the other one.' You can also try this with a coin. Remember, it's not the way the coin lands that is important: it is your internal reaction that you pay attention to.

'Identity parade'

To be truly happy and healthy we also need to understand ourselves. This means exploring our identity, beliefs and skills.

Our identity is about who we are. We sometimes say, 'I'm just not that kind of person'; 'The course/job I do is just not me.'

We instinctively know who we are. We need to know consciously who we are. Our type can give us clues.

The following list of roles can also help identify which roles 'are you'. Look at them now. Which are you drawn to?

Roles	Roles	Roles	Roles
artist	leader	adviser	leader
athlete	learner	advocate	follower
inventor	magician	artist	provider
discoverer	mediator	coach	student
comedian	warrior	doctor	teacher
explorer friend	parent	engineer	visionary
hero/heroine	victim	entrepreneur	writer
hunter			
performer			

Another way to find your identity is to list people you admire (Robbie Williams, Einstein, Madonna, Mother Teresa?) and write down what it is you admire about them. These are likely to be the qualities through which you can develop your own unique identity.

From our identity we take our beliefs and values. There are things we believe we can and can't do. Beliefs are important because they often determine whether we will try something new, risk learning new things or stay where we are. If we learn something new we acquire a new skill. Skills usually develop through practice. Once we have mastered a skill we then believe we can do it regularly. Skills can be opening doors, playing an instrument, drawing and fishing. What are your skills?

Young children love developing skills. Colouring in pictures without going over the lines is something we all learn. First, we need to believe we can. Encouragement from adults usually imprints the belief. Then continual practice improves the skill until it becomes behaviour.

We can change our behaviour more easily than our personality. It is best to criticise someone's behaviour rather than his or her skills, beliefs or identity.

For example, which of these criticisms would you prefer if you left your bedroom in a mess?

- You didn't tidy your bedroom this morning! (Behaviour)
- You didn't tidy your bedroom properly! (Skill)
- You don't understand how important it is to contribute to keeping the house tidy! (Value)
- You are a selfish person because you didn't tidy your bedroom this morning! (Identity)

It is best to criticise behaviour because it is easiest to change and does not damage someone's self-esteem.

Some people earn lots of money but are unhappy. This is usually because they are using their skills but are not living by their beliefs or identity. You need to get *all* of them to be really happy.

Tip: Start from identity, then beliefs, to skills, to behaviour – not the other way.

The best of *S* and *N*

> '*Nine out of ten of my experiments fail, and that is considered a pretty good record amongst scientists.*'
> **Professor Sir Harold Kato, chemist and Nobel laureate**

This quotation highlights the value of both $S+$ and $N+$.

$S+$, keep on going, despite setbacks, looking at the detailed results.

$N+$, keep thinking of new solutions until you find the answer.

The best of *N*

Developing *N*+ is about imagining positive goals and dreaming great dreams, about who we can become or how we can solve problems by dreaming up new ideas. It is when our minds move from the conscious level (when the brain uses beta waves – great for *S*+ thinking) and moves to alpha waves – great for *N*+ thinking. This process happens naturally every forty minutes or so, when the brain seems to move from beta to alpha for at least a short time.

Great creative thinkers stay in the creative dreamy state for longer.

Einstein would go on long walks of up to twelve hours.

Leonardo Da Vinci, inventor and artist, said, 'I stop sometimes and look in to the flames of a fire, or clouds, or mud, or listen to the sounds of bells and find really marvellous things!'

Our best ideas come from this approach. It is called many things – image streaming, imagination, creative spark, daydreaming. The result is new ideas, inventions and works of art. So, when you used to stare out of the window during a lesson you found dull, you were using *N* behaviour!

Develop your *N* thinking by focusing on the outcome you'd like and how good you will feel once you are there. Use the motto, 'We could try this.' Use words such as achieve, *gain, have, possibilities*, new and goals when encouraging others to use *N* behaviour.

I'll sleep on it

Dreams often help us solve problems creatively. This is probably why people with a problem will often say, 'I'll sleep on it.'

Elias Howe was an inventor. He was trying to invent the sewing machine. Nothing worked. One night he had a terrible nightmare in which cannibals were chasing him. Their gleaming spears had an eye-shaped hole near the tip. He woke up sweating and scared, but he knew he had discovered the answer to his sewing-machine problem. All human progress started in someone's imagination. What's inside yours?

Thinking like children

Another way to develop *N*+ is to think more like children. Einstein said he solved problems by thinking like a child. He meant forget the rules you're supposed to know so they don't get in the way. This is why he said imagination is more important than knowledge.

Children love to play. A fidget of five-year-olds can learn so much through play because they are honest, laugh, move around and are curious – and so can teenagers and adults.

Nobel prizes for laughter

Every year alternative Nobel prizes are awarded to scientists involved in research that makes us laugh. Recently, researchers have discovered which animals can shoot poo out of their bottom the furthest! And two researchers, one an Olympic swimming hopeful, wondered if you could swim faster in water or custard. What do you think? The answers are at the bottom of the page.

Thinking differently

Someone once said, 'If you think there is only one answer then you will only find one.'

Challenge: Write BUZZ on four small bits of paper. Can you line them up so you can read BUZZ ten times? The answer is at the end of the book on Page 152.

Answers to questions on previous page: (a) penguin (if humans were as good, we'd be able to shoot our poo over a garden fence – probably just as well we can't or gardening would be far less popular and relaxing!); (b) swimmers through both custard and water achieve exactly the same speeds (the experiment was designed to assess the effect of pull and drag forces on swimmers). Source: *New Scientist Magazine*.

Here is a game you can use to develop *N+*, 'Time Travel'.

'Time travel'

Imagine you are going to attend a school reunion in five years' time. If you'd rather choose a youth club, family or other get-together, that's fine. Write down the date exactly five years from now in the star below. Imagine yourself five years from now. Imagine the five years have gone really well – the best they could possibly be. Write down in the star what has happened to you. What have you achieved? How do you look? What are you wearing? How do you feel? What work are you doing? Where do you live? What are the best things you could hear people say about you? Take at least five minutes. Let your imagination run wild! Read the list. How good does it feel to have achieved these things? What are the three most important things?

Rewrite these on a small piece of card or paper inside a star shape, dated five years from today. Keep the list somewhere safe. Remember the three things and promise yourself you will move towards them. If your list doesn't excite you and make you feel really good, try it again – dream bigger dreams!

Alyson recently imagined her future. She hadn't thought about it before. Her dream is to be a hairdresser to the stars. When she wrote it down she felt really good and excited. So good she wanted to make sure it happened. She started to think about small practical things she could do to move towards her dream. Her attendance at school improved. She has fixed up a Saturday job in a trendy hairdressing salon.

ALYSON'S STAR

Step 1: Date: 1/9/2011
Step 2: My Job
☆ Hairdresser to the stars
☆ Live in my own flat in Newcastle near my friends
☆ Have a really fit Boyfriend
Step 3: 1. Go to College
2. Get a Saturday Job
3. Look in the papers at flats
4. Check out with friends who would like to move in with me:- JOANNE, AMY, MATT?
Step 4: ADVICE: GO FOR IT!
(Don't waste time)

What future would you like?

Fun Game –make your future into a song, choose a style; rap, rock, heavy, pop. Verse 1 should be about you now, verses 2 and 3 you 5 years later having achieved your dreams, use the advice (step 4) to make your chorus.

The best of *S*

Developing *S* is about taking care of the details, to make sure our big dreams and ideas (*N+*) actually happen. This way of behaving is really useful to overcome short-term problems, perhaps when there is an accident or emergency. It makes sure the important steps are identified and sorted. People naturally good at this are usually list makers: they have shopping lists, things-to-do-today lists, even lists about their lists!

To develop *S+* use words and phrases such as obstacles, problems, avoid, exclude and get rid of. *S+* is about identifying all of the issues and problems that need to be answered after the *N+* thinking has created the big ideas and possibilities. Both approaches together get better results than using just one. It is said that Walt Disney used this approach – *N+* first, then *S+* – to develop many of his best ideas. When we use *S+* we see the detail first and 'move upwards; and when we use *N+* we see the big picture first and then 'move down' towards the detail. Here is a game you can use to develop *S+* behaviour:

'Happy list'

Write down below all the things you do that really make you happy. (Spend at least four whole minutes.)

_____   _____   _____

_____   _____   _____

_____   _____   _____

_____   _____   _____

_____   _____   _____

_____   _____   _____

The best of *F* and *T*

Exploring your *F* and *T* behaviour can be very useful.

When we talk, we reveal how our minds and bodies actually experience things and make sense of the world around us. Have you ever been 'in the thick of things' or felt you were 'miles away'?

When we're in a situation, we can throw ourselves into it, completely absorbed by the experience, like watching a great film and feeling as if we're totally immersed or involved, forgetting the time and place. We drink in the sights, sounds, smells and atmosphere and feel it completely. We usually experience things as big, loud, bright and bold. We remember things well this way. We are associated into an experience. This can be good when we're enjoying a film, tasty food, football match, or bad when we remember a visit to the dentist, a phobia or giving someone unpleasant news. This is using *F* behaviour.

When revising for exams, associate fully into your work. Create a memorable experience by enjoying the signs, sounds, smells and feeling while you revise. You'll remember more!

The alternative is to be *dissociated*. This is when we're not really there. Our minds have wandered off somewhere else in a daydream to somewhere more pleasing. We usually experience the present as vague and blurred. We therefore remember details poorly when we try to recall them later. We usually dissociate when we're bored because our mind thinks, 'Oh, no, this is so boring – I'm going somewhere else.' This is using our *T*. This can be useful, e.g. when you are going to experience something potentially unpleasant (doctors, dentists, exams). We can dissociate from our body and move away from the unpleasant feelings, sights, sounds. Magicians who can lie on a bed of nails without feeling any pain use this technique. If you have to tell someone something unpleasant, imagine you are watching yourself telling them from a camera about 6 metres away. You can also use this to move away from negative emotions such as anger and sadness.

Being 'dissociated' can be bad when we need to be paying attention to the present situation.

Practice both *F* and *T* by reading these two stories. One will make you use *F* behaviour and the other *T* behaviour. Can you guess which is which?

1. Imagine standing in the corner of a room looking through the viewfinder of a video camera. What you see is in black and white. You can see a door in the distance, which opens. In comes someone looking a bit like you. A small child, whom you've never seen before, holds a grey bowl near the door. The person

115

takes something from the bowl. You notice the child is giggling and adjust the focus to make the picture clearer. As you do, they both look into the camera.

2. What colour is your front door? Imagine you are standing outside of your front door now in bare feet. On which side of the door is the handle? Left or right? Imagine it is really cold outside and your toes are freezing as you touch the cold handle now and push open the door. Feel a wall of heat as you step inside. Feel your feet on the warm, soft carpet. Pick up a sweet in a blue wrapper from a gold bowl held by a small child you've never seen before and put it in your mouth now. Start sucking it and feel it touch your tongue and the insides of your teeth. It tastes of lemon, a very strong taste of lemon juice, and rhubarb. Now the taste is changing to your favourite food. Mmm! Taste it now. You look at the child, who is giggling as only children can, an infectious, warm, happy laugh. The child played a trick on you and is really pleased. Feel how happy the child feels, imagine the scene from its point of view, remember laughing like a child yourself until your sides hurt. And then you notice a friendly figure standing about 3 metres away from you both, holding a small silver video recorder.

Start to use both *F* and *T* for increased flexibility of behaviour. Can you think of some useful situations in which you can use these behaviours?

Here are two games you can play that help develop both: 'Role modelling' and 'Energy bubble'.

'Role modelling'

1. Relax and get comfortable in your seat. Think of someone you admire, someone who is relaxed, confident, liked and well thought of by most people.

2. Imagine the person in front of you now. See their face smile at you. You can learn from them now. They are ready to help you. Imagine floating inside their body now. Feel what it feels like as you stretch into their body. Feel your feet in theirs and your fingers inside theirs. See and hear the world through their eyes and ears. What makes them so good? How do they stand, walk, talk, and look at a person that is different to your way. Notice the tiny details they do differently. Remember these so you can use them later to be more confident and relaxed, more able to influence other people positively. When you have learned everything, you can step outside their body and back into yours.

In the legend of King Arthur, Merlin taught Arthur many things by turning him into animals, such as a fish and a bird. When asked what he learned as a bird, Arthur said that from the sky England did not have borders. When he became King this inspired him to make England a united kingdom. This is learning through empathy – the best of *F*.

People naturally good at *T* often 'play back' conversations they've had with other people as if they were watching it happen on a TV screen. This is useful because you can analyse the scene without getting upset or too involved. It can also help you understand the other person's point of view.

'Energy bubble'

Imagine that you have a bubble of energy projecting out from your central point and surrounding you like a sort of science-fiction force field. Everything stressful that happens outside this bubble just bounces off and away from you, leaving you calm and still inside the bubble. So, the more stressful it is outside, the calmer you are inside. Imagine harsh words bouncing off so they can't get inside you. Imagine the field protecting you in your favourite colour.

There is not really a bubble of energy around you, but your unconscious mind doesn't distinguish between imagination and 'reality' – think about chewing tin foil now! So if you imagine that you are shielded from stress, you will be! This is another good one for pressure situations.

Another way

Being able to see things through your own eyes and also the eyes of the person you're talking to is very useful. A third viewpoint is to imagine watching you and the other person talking. This can help you see things differently. This is a good way to see solutions that could satisfy both of you, not just one of you. We do all of this naturally when watching films and TV; sometimes we identify with one character, then another and sometimes more than one.

The best of *J* and *P*

By exploring how we talk to ourselves, we can develop the best of *J* and *P*.

Thirty years ago, you might have been locked up for admitting hearing voices in your head. Although some people still are, it is accepted that we all talk to ourselves.

This can be positive ('Come on, come on, I can do it, yes!') or negative ('You can't ask for a refund: you'd be so embarrassed.'). By recognising and exposing the ways we talk negatively to ourselves, which prevent us achieving our potential and doing our best, we can either ignore the negativity or answer it back and tell it that it's wrong! If a friend talked to us in the way we talk to ourselves, they wouldn't be our friend for very long.

Here are some of the 'tricks' used by our negative/critical voice and tips on how we can change the voice to a more useful one. Which ones are your favourites!

1. Positively negative

Dwelling only on the negative: If you are given four positive comments and one negative, you will run through the negative comment over and over again.

Ignoring the positive: Writing off a good performance as a fluke, luck or someone else's work, e.g. 'Well it wasn't really me, it was … lucky … helped by someone.'

Do you use this voice?

Yes ☐

No ☐

Give an example: _____

_____

_____

Try reversing these, to build up the positive and shrink the negative.

How could you change the words?

Write down a positive alternative and read it to yourself three times, e.g. 'I did really well, it was down to me.'

_____

_____

_____

2. Generalising for poor behaviour

Describing events in simple black-or-white terms and concluding the worst: You might snap, 'My friend said something negative to me so nobody will ever be my friend again'; 'I failed that interview, so I'll never get a job/place at college' etc.

Do you use this voice?

Yes ☐

No ☐

Give an example: _____

_____

_____

Try win–win instead: 'I gained interview practice, which will help me get an even better job.'

How could you change the words?

Write down a positive alternative and read it to yourself three times.

_____

_____

_____

3. Low self-esteem labelling

Rating yourself or others in a bad way. Instead of recognising that you need to improve some skills, you write yourself off as a complete failure. Your voice says, 'You're a complete idiot.' Are you sure, 100% of the time, or just in the mornings? One failing does not mean you always fail. Unhelpful labels include, 'She's always late,' 'he doesn't care about anyone but himself.'

Do you use this voice?

Yes ☐

No ☐

Give an example: _____

_____

_____

Focus on what you or the other person can do to minimise the chance of a repetition.

How could you change the words?

Write down a positive alternative and read it to yourself three times.

_____

_____

_____

4. Shoulds, musts and oughts

The words we use to give ourselves commands and the way we say them determines our *J* or *P* behaviour. Those who listen to their voices and do what they're told are usually *J*-preference people. Those who ignore their 'should' voices are often *P* preferences. Imposing upon yourself and others rigid unreasonable standards is an easy way for you to increase stress. When you say, 'I must, I should, I ought', you are not allowing yourself choice or control over your actions. This is OK when you say, 'I must not put my hand in the fire' – but check out each *must, should* and *ought* you use. You must keep only the useful ones, shouldn't you?

Must you keep your bedroom clean after you've broken your leg or could you let your standards slip for a day or two?

Do you use this voice? (*must, should, ought to*)

Yes ☐

No ☐

Give an example: _____

_____

_____

Beware of starting sentences with 'I must', 'I should' or 'I ought'. Instead, step back and allow yourself to take and enjoy control and choice.

How could you change the words? ('I could do it now' or 'I could do it later'.)

Write down a positive alternative and read it to yourself three times.

_____

_____

_____

Replace phrases such as 'You make me …', 'I can't stand it …', and 'I can never …' with phrases that allow at least a glimpse of your overcoming the thing that annoys you.

A simple way to beat your negative voice is to imagine it as an annoying, squeaky or other silly voice, e.g. the Crazy Frog. You are far less likely to take the negative comment seriously if it is made by a 'silly' voice. Or you could imagine the voice as an animal or person you don't take seriously. If a small tortoise is sitting on your shoulder telling you off, you're not as likely to feel so bad. This is generally good advice when *J*-preference behaviour is unhelpful.

For the times we're using *P* behaviour and are not able to motivate ourselves, perhaps we could talk to ourselves in a strict army-sergeant voice.

For example, when you're lying in bed and it's a Saturday morning and you say to yourself in a sleepy, tired, calm voice, 'Oh, this is a nice lie-in, I'm all snugly and warm and I *could* get up,' you'll probably stay in bed. If you suddenly realise it's a Friday and you should be in school or at work in seven minutes' time, your internal voice will probably change to, 'Get up, now, quick, *you must*, or you'll be late' – and you'll be out of bed straightaway.

Start listening to your voices, and remember that you can change them.

Role model wanted

Find yourself a role model. Your best role model is you. Befriend yourself. Start listening to the positive voices inside (and around) you. Start asking yourself what you want to achieve. If our friends spoke to us in the way we speak to ourselves, they probably wouldn't be our friends; we would not take their criticism. So why take it from ourselves?

What would you do if you knew you couldn't fail?

Listening to and changing the words can really help you buzz.

Now, bringing in very good ones is one very good thing you can do now.

The best of – (negative)

It may seem strange at first, but we can use negative experiences and feelings to help move us forward in a positive direction.

Richard Branson is quoted as saying he has learned far more from his mistakes than from his successes, and success tends to follow such an attitude. Most successful businesspeople share Richard Branson's attitude. It's not failure: it's feedback. Fear of failure freezes us. Failure can spur us on to try new things.

How to grow a go for it attitude!

- Do some silly things.
- Learn to prefer the risk of embarrassment more than the risk of freezing – examples to try with some friends:
    - dance somewhere without music playing;
    - walk like penguins (not the other thing penguins do really well);
    - do your best sheep impressions;
    - don't try them all at once (unless you want a really good attitude)!

Most of our fears are never realised. If we keep imaging the worst that could happen, it probably won't, but we'll feel bad until we *know* it won't, or feel bad when it does. We can't change our past – only how we remember it. Neither should we worry about what could go wrong – instead make sure we're planning to make things go well!

Here is a game that can help turn negative thoughts around: 'Fear fighting'.

'Fear Fighting'

1. Think of the fears you'd like to learn from. Do them one at a time. (You could choose fear of failure, of ill health, of having no friends.)
2. Think about the fear for a moment. Experience the feelings that go with this.

122

3. Now ask yourself, 'What could the benefit for that fear be? What could my inner voice be wanting me to know that will have a positive effect on me?' You may notice more than one positive. Accept those that feel right.

4. Thank your inner voice

5. Now act upon the advice and the fear has become a help.

Example: Fear of ill health for John:

Positive inner voice: 1. Stop overeating!

2. Just get on with your life, stop wasting time on a course you know you don't like!

Action for John: healthy eating and change of course (instead of worrying about ill health and not liking the course).

The best of + (positive)

Developing the best of positive behaviour has many benefits, many already described throughout *The Buzz*. Which are your favourites so far?

Here is another that creates a background feel-good buzz of happiness and charisma that spreads not only around your body but projects outwards, making other people feel good too! It's called 'The Buzz'.

Buzzing is called loads of things that all mean feeling absolutely brilliant – *flow, in the zone, kicking ass, walking on air, ten feet tall, hot stuff ...*

If we all spent more time here, our world would be full of people as amazing and as beautiful as the world itself can be.

'The Buzz'

1. Think of a time you felt really confident, a time you felt in control, as if you could achieve whatever you wanted to, when you felt happy and good.

2. Give this feeling a name such as 'buzzing', 'winning', 'go for it'. Add a colour, such as blue, or whatever sums up the great feeling that you feel. Add a piece of upbeat music you really like – the theme from *Rocky*, *Superman* or *Wonder Woman* or a track by your favourite band. Imagine the sound blasting out from speakers the size of a bus.

3. Now, remember in detail this time you felt really confident. Go back and re-member what you could see, hear and feel. Notice where the feeling starts in your body and where it goes. Notice the speed and temperature of the feeling. What words do you hear? Make the pictures, sounds and feelings bigger, brighter, louder, faster, stronger until you feel very good. Keep doing this until you feel fantastic. Keep going until you feel a 'high'. When you do, capture this feeling by pressing your thumb and forefinger together or use any of the other anchor techniques we discussed on Page 89.

4. You can check it works by pressing your thumb and forefinger together later. The feeling will return. If not, repeat until it does work.

5. Use this whenever you need to feel confident or just to feel good all of the time.

Section Three

Go For It

Section Three
Go For It

Have you noticed how evil villains always want to take over the world or universe?

They want to control everything and everyone. Lex Luther, Darth Vader, they're all at it. They just want to be liked.

The best way to achieve this is to like yourself first. Discover your strengths, take control of your behaviour and then go for it. This is much easier than taking over the world or universe, which wouldn't leave much spare time for hobbies and interests. This is probably why we never saw Darth Vader playing tennis or sunbathing.

When successful people are asked to give advice, they usually say the same thing. Go for it. When people in old folk's homes are asked, 'What advice would you give young people?' they say the same thing: go for it.

Potty advice?

Sarah, aged 26, was on a course I was delivering. She had always wanted to set up her own business selling Italian money pots. You save coins in them and, as there is no hole in the base, you have to break the pot at the top when it's full. A wish is said to come true when you break the pot! You're left with the money you saved, a decorative pot for plants and a wish, all for about £10.

Sarah's grandfather was very ill and in hospital. She visited him and told him of her dream. She'd always been very close to him as a child. What do you think he said?

His advice was, 'Go for it, do not hesitate any longer.' Don't lie in a bed; don't die in a bed when you're old wishing you'd done this or that. Listen to your head and heart and do it. Put all of your energy into it and be your best.

Do set yourself positive goals and move towards them with the best of all ten of the chunks of behaviour you've learned in *The Buzz* so far. Do enjoy going for it. In some goals you'll succeed; in some you'll exceed; and in others things will turn out differently – you can change them on the way.

People who go for it tend to achieve more of what they want.

They say that eventually they feel as if they're swimming with the tide. A positive direction with positive action and things start to go our way. Swimming against the tide in a negative direction is hopeless.

Buzzing in action: time to buzz

Buzzing in 1973

Feeling great and buzzing is something we all do. But some people don't do it enough. I asked one group of adults I was training to think of a time they felt buzzing, great, fantastic, a time they felt everything was going their way. One woman seemed to be really struggling to remember such a time. I encouraged her until she smiled and nodded, indicating she had remembered a great time. 'Fantastic,' I said, 'When was it?'

'Nineteen seventy-three,' she replied.

Wow, some people feel good only once every thirty years or so! This is not enough. Let's be greedy. We can feel good whenever we need to feel good now, ten times a day, even twenty. It costs nothing, so go for it. Feeling good makes us happier and healthier, rubs off on people around us and is as quick as feeling bad.

Here are seven great ways to buzz. Try as many as you need for now, and then more.

Practise your chocolate voice (see Page 105 and *Go for it or buzzing* Page 83) before using these.

Seven ways to be your best

1. Buzz when chatting to people you fancy.
2. Buzz at sport.
3. Buzz when talking to groups.
4. Buzz while learning more.
5. Melt away stress and relax.
6. Buzz with confidence in the present.
7. Buzz with confidence about your future.

I really fancy you

Copping off, spinning, tapping off, pulling – it has many different names but the situation is the same. Surveys suggest that seven out of every ten people are hopeless at talking to people they fancy. Are you? If so, you can learn from those who do it well. There is no need ever to miss out talking to people you fancy: just copy those who do it well.

Panda seeks love

There's no excuse for not being able to find a partner who will love you and treat you well. If you're a panda there is an excuse. They are an endangered species; there aren't many of them. A panda could go for days without meeting another panda. Even buzzing, they might not find a partner. But there are billions of humans on this planet. Even if only one out of every hundred people in your age group fancies you, there will be 23 million people out there just hoping you'll talk to them because they find you gorgeous. So many people, so few days – hesitation is not an option.

And here's *how* to. As soon as you see someone you fancy and have decided you'd like to talk to them, try these five steps:

Step 1

Say something positive to yourself, in your chocolate voice, such as, 'I can talk to them, they could really like me, and we could get on very well.'

Step 2

Picture the two of you talking together in four minutes' time.

Picture it in detail: you're both smiling, you're both having a great time, laughing, enjoying each other's company.

Imagine they are attracted to you, and how good that makes you feel. Notice the feeling of confidence and curiosity grow, and enjoy it.

Step 3

Hear them say, 'I really fancy you, I like you, you're interesting, funny and gorgeous.'

Repeat at least three times.

Step 4

While feeling in that go for it mood, say to yourself, 'I'm going to talk to them and, if they don't fancy me, I don't mind: there are 23 million others who will fancy me.'

Step 5

Before you go over and talk to them, repeat Steps 2 and 3 until you feel the irresistible and strong force compelling you to approach the person you fancy.

Now have fun – you are alive!

Probably not everyone will fancy you

John, aged seventeen, said to me he'd been using this technique but he still didn't have a girl-friend. The technique does not mean everyone you talk to will fancy you. It means you will be able to approach everyone you fancy. There is a difference!

Life would probably be boring, anyway, if everyone fancied you. There would be no fun and excitement in life if everyone fancied you, hundreds of people following you around every-where making gooey faces at you! This technique guarantees that the people you approach will see you at your best, buzzing. This gives you your best chance of success.

One girl told me she is physically sick when she sees someone she really fancies!

I don't think she'll be showing off her best qualities to a lad if she's showering him in sick as she approaches! Better to use the above 'I fancy you' approach, perhaps.

Be your best at sport

Top sports performers have some things in common.

As well as ability, they also stick to the following routine. By using it you will be your best during the sporting activity. It does not matter if it is football, tennis, swimming, athletics, basketball or martial arts: the process is the same. People with great ability who don't have a version of this routine never fulfil their full potential.

Just before the event or game follow these three steps:

Step 1

Look at your opponents and say to yourself, in your chocolate voice, 'I can beat you.'

Look for a potential weakness: they may be too big to balance well or too small to outpower you.

Step 2

Say, 'I will do my best' inside and imagine doing really well.

Notice how it feels when you're on top form, how your body moves, and seems to know what to do almost automatically.

Step 3

Now feel go for it, strongly.

Repeat all three steps and build a powerfully positive mood.

Until you are ready to go and do your best, enjoy it – this is living; this is buzzing.

Boxing clever

Muhammad Ali was one of the world's greatest ever boxers. He followed a routine similar to this. He called Step 2 'future histories'. He would imagine in vivid detail his forthcoming fight, the great moves he would make, the punches and blocks he would make. Ability and confidence go well together.

'I can' or 'I will'?

One girl said to me, 'I say, "I will win", not, "I can win" and "I'll do my best". Surely my words are better.'

Can you guess why they are not?

I asked if she always won. She said no.

'How do you feel when you don't win?' I asked.

She looked sad and said, 'Awful, annoyed, disappointed and angry with myself.'

'For how long?' I asked.

'Oh, for a couple of days.'

'Then what?'

'I suppose I say to myself that I did my best and I start to look forward to my next race.' She shrugged.

This is why her words are not as good as 'I can win'.

If she changes her words, she will perform just as well but not feel bad for a 'couple of days' when she doesn't win. Also, when she does win, it will feel better. Can you guess why?

Motivation for sports training

Some people train long and hard for their sport. We read about swimmers getting up at 5 a.m. to swim at a local pool, even in the freezing winter months. These people normally motivate themselves by using a mixture of 'away-from' and 'towards' motivation. They picture themselves winning medals or trophies, hear the applause of the crowd and feel the pride of winning to motivate them to train hard. They also imagine some negative worth avoiding, saying things such as, 'I don't want to look back and think I didn't give it my best shot, thinking if I'd not missed training sessions I'd have a gold instead of a fourth place.' Try a bit of both to motivate yourself.

Talking in front of groups

Some say, 'I'd rather die or stroke a spider than talk in front of groups!'

In surveys, the fear of presenting is usually ranked higher than the fear of death, spiders and sharks! It needn't be. Whether you have to present a project or report to an audience or perform in an interview for a job or course, you can do so buzzing. This will ensure your audience has as great a time as you do.

Before your talk, event or interview, use these three steps:

Step 1

Get the go for it feeling going and growing inside you. Feel it strongly.

Mmm! Use your chocolate voice.

Step 2

When you speak, imagine the buzzing feeling coming out of your mouth as a mist in your favourite colour, gently moving out and over the heads of your audience and back down, and pull it back through your audience and back into your legs and up through your body again. Feel it as the coloured mist and keep it circulating. Fill it with warmth and caring, a feeling that you and the audience are all here to have a great time and enjoy yourselves. Have fun, enjoy yourself. This is living; this is buzzing.

Step 3

Continue the feeling until just after you've finished the session, and then relax.

Stage fright

Someone wanted to be a confident speaker, so they asked a great speaker, 'What can I do to get rid of the butterflies in my stomach before I'm due to speak?'

'Don't get rid of them,' came the reply. 'Learn stage flight.'

'What's that?'

'Stage flight is the art of getting the butterflies to fly in formation and into your audience, filling their hearts with the beautiful colours of the butterflies' wings.'

Learning more

Some people who have studied how we learn have found that we can understand more during our learning and revision, and recall more of it during exams and tests, if we enter a learning state.

The learning state

Sometimes we learn really well. At other times things seem to fly in one ear and out of the other. Would you like to be able to learn really well when you want to? The learning state can help you remember twice as much as you do normally.

Luckily, it is quite easy to get into the learning state.

1. Familiarise yourself with the room in which you'll be learning. Look around it and notice a few details – colours, shapes, objects.
2. Look at a small object directly in front of you. It could be something on a wall, the back of a chair, anything fairly small towards which you can direct your focus.
3. Now, without moving your eyes, become aware of your peripheral vision. Notice things at the corner of your eyes without shifting your gaze. Slowly start to imagine and see things that are at your side, by your ears, as you stay focused on the object/thing in front of you.
4. Now imagine pulling your awareness right round and behind – see behind you in your mind's eye. You may imagine stepping out of your body and being able to see the whole room. Remember the object and detail you saw at the beginning.

You are now in the learning state. Your awareness is heightened. This can be a useful technique to 'anchor' and to use during exams, revision and lessons you'd particularly like to remember. Beware: your performance can dramatically improve if you use this technique. Try it only if you're prepared for better performance!

Relax and remove stress

Being able to relax deeply is of great benefit to all of us.

It is particularly good to use when you've become great at buzzing with excitement and go for it. You can use relaxation to recharge your batteries and help heal your body in the most natural way when you relax deeply and slow down your breathing and reading without even knowing you're doing it, and then melt away all the tension from all of your muscles, from the tip of your head all the way down and out through your toes, washed away, reinvigorating your muscles with the potential for power and strength.

In which part of your body do you have most tension? It is different for each of us. Some like to lose tension from their face first, others to lose tension from their shoulders and others to lose all the tension from their belly. Imagine how good we can all feel when even this tension has melted away, leaving us as relaxed as a baby sleeping deeply and dreaming in a safe and comfortable place. We all relaxed when we were babies and we can remember if we just let go for long enough.

You could put on some relaxing music while reading the 'relaxometer' (see below).

How relaxed are you before reading the relaxometer on a scale of 1 to10 (1 = feeling totally chilled; 10 = feeling totally stressed out)?

Check afterwards what happens to your score to find how effective it can be. Keep using it and you'll get more benefit; keep using it until you get down to 1. It takes most people four attempts over four days to achieve this.

The relaxometer

Sit comfortably in your chair and begin to relax. Take a deep breath in and, as you breathe out, release any tension from your body. Repeat, and on each out breath feel any tension, stress and hassle leave your whole body. Any tension trapped in your shoulders, neck or anywhere else just melts away, gone, leaving you relaxing more and more. Now think of a place you enjoy relaxing: in bed, on a beach or in a favourite place you like to be.

Now slightly defocus your eyes and really imagine being there now. See what you can see and hear what you can hear as you remember your special place, as you continue to relax more and more, all the way down, feeling lighter as you drift further and further. See, hear and feel what it's like, relaxing in the place you are, as you relax so deeply that all the tension has completely dissolved away, gone, vanished, leaving you feeling so clean and fresh, ready for the good feelings, ready to make the most of all the positive things that you can experience and enjoy more because when you are really relaxed you can easily choose to face in a positive direction, looking towards all the positive dreams, hopes, moods and experiences you can have. And they are all there for you.

When you relax, you face in a positive direction. Notice how good this feels because this is the direction in which you are and you become your best, the direction in which you achieve everything you want from life: happiness, health and love.

The inevitable frustrations of life won't knock you off course – in fact, they will only strengthen your inner resolve towards your best future.

Now, as you absorb all this new information so that it becomes part of your thinking, you can begin to come back from the relaxation you've enjoyed, come back to being alert and awake, refreshed and ready to remember the eyes-opening experience you've enjoyed. As you fully bring your conscious attention back into this place, have a little stretch and feel good, remembering how good it is to relax and learn more about yourself.

Self-esteem builder

'It's never too late to be what you might have been'

George Elliot

Strong positive self-esteem is the rock on which we build our health and happiness. Negative self-esteem usually leads to negative behaviour. Self-esteem is what we feel when we think about ourselves. Positive self-esteem provides us with strength, confidence and inner reserves, allowing us to achieve our best. Positive self-esteem is what makes us a good leader, inspiring those around us to do more than they thought possible.

Would you like to create a strong positive self-esteem for yourself?

To measure the increase in your self-esteem, rate where it is now, on a scale of 1 to 10 (1 = very poor; 10 = very good). Rate it again after you have finished the game. People who do this a number of times get the best results.

Successful people do their self-esteem in the following way:

1. Think of someone you love or admire (parent, boyfriend or girlfriend, pop star). See their face and hear them say to you, 'I love you, you're brilliant.' Keep replaying their words, seeing the love in their eyes, feeling the warmth of their love until it sinks deep inside of you and makes you feel loved and special. See their face like a small picture about 15 centimetres in front of, but slightly above, your left eye. Imagine their love travelling through their words into you like a mist in your favourite colour.

2. Think of a skill or quality you have. Something you know you're good at. Perhaps you're a really kind person or are really good at drawing or football. Think of a time you knew this to be true. Pretend to go there now and make a picture of it, add sounds to it and feel how good it felt that moment you knew you were good at it. Enjoy the feeling, and place the picture in front of you next to the last one, and imagine the same coloured mist coming out of that memory and into your body filling it with the good feelings.

3. Think of something you'd like to achieve in the future. A goal or ambition that is important to you. How will you know when you've achieved it? Think about how good you'll feel when you've achieved it. Think of a picture that shows you have achieved your goal, it could be you with a beautiful partner, with or without children, or in a great job or in a big car – whatever picture shows you have achieved your goal. Place the picture about 15 centimetres in front of, but slightly above, your right eye. Feel the great feeling of success and happiness flow towards you as the warm mist of your favourite colour. Enjoy it as it fills your body.

4. Now, whenever you think of yourself, bring those three pictures up in front of you and enjoy breathing in the love, confidence, warmth and satisfaction from the memories. Remember to put the pictures slightly above your eye line so you look up a bit when you see them. Practise until it becomes natural, and your self-esteem will shoot up!

What number would you like your self-esteem to reach? Keep practicing until you at least reach that number.

The amoeba – a simple life-form

Amoebae are simple life-forms. They move away from bad things (toxins, things that are too hot, too cold) and move towards good things (food). Perhaps we could learn from them. Do we sometimes take ourselves too seriously? It is said that 80 per cent of our thoughts are the ones we have every day, circulating around and around. So we should make sure they're good positive thoughts, otherwise our thoughts will be like the stale air that goes round and round within a badly ventilated building where someone could fart on a Monday and you could still be breathing it on Friday, for the thirtieth time! Open the window of your mind and let in some fresh new thoughts.

Bringing more laughter into your life is a great way to feel better about yourself. When we laugh, people laugh with us.

Laughter versus stress

Laughter is also a great alternative to stress. A good laugh out loud produces health benefits, such as increased oxygen in the blood and a release of endorphins (those happy chemicals that can stop a virus wriggling into our cells, as well as relieving pain). It's also good exercise. We can use every muscle group in our body if we laugh well enough. Has your homework task ever been to go and have a really good laugh? If not, try it tonight. Share the funniest moments you've ever had, the most embarrassing things you've ever said and done, those funny family stories you've heard a hundred times but always make you laugh until tears stream down your face.

Laughter is also great because it shows us as we really are, and that it is OK because we're all basically the same, especially when we're laughing. Laughter is said to be the shortest distance between two people. That's when we do have a better life than an amoeba!

Do these real signs and headlines make you laugh?

Bargain Basement – upstairs.

Toilet out of order – please use floor below.

We repair anything – please knock as doorbell broken.

Open 7 days a week – except Mondays.

Thinking in a happy direction

Are the following helpful ways of thinking? What do you think they could mean to you?

'There is no such thing as bad weather, just wrong clothing'
Billy Connolly, comedian

'Some people light up a room when they enter it and others when they leave it
Oscar Wilde

'The trouble with being in the rat race is that even if you win you're still a rat'
Lily Tomlin, actress

A visit to the cinema

I've heard it said that we all have at least one good idea for a song and a film inside of us. Now's your chance to explore it.

By working your way through *The Buzz,* you now have a good idea about your natural strengths. Maybe you've already turned this into goals – a course, career or something else.

I'd like you to imagine having your own personal cinema. Imagine sitting in a really comfortable seat now. Think of the colour of it and the smell you'd like in your private cinema. Perhaps the faint smell of popcorn or chocolate as you look up to a huge screen in front of you. The surround speakers are bigger than buses. Now, on this screen will play the movie of your life for the next ten years – which is Part 1 of a long-running series. This movie is going to be the best feel-good movie ever – because you are the one person it will make feel really good!

In the movie you are the main character and you'll become the best you that you can be.

In a moment you'll see the final scene of the film, which shows you've had a brilliant ten years, the best you can imagine. You've made it happen by using all of the natural strengths and talents you have and all of the new behaviours you have learned about and then used from *The Buzz.* So it is not a lottery win: it is success you've fully earned and deserved through planning and working hard towards it. Most movies are about an hour and a half, but you can make yours a bit longer or a bit shorter.

So focus on this last scene now. What have you achieved? How do you look? Where are you? Who is with you? Where do you live? Fill in as much detail as you can. Don't merely see yourself on the screen with the colours big, bright and bold, but hear the encouraging words of those around you, hear some of your favourite go for it music and blast the inspirational sound through the huge speakers so you can hear and see your success as you begin to feel it more and more. How do you feel seeing yourself look at this scene and making it as vivid and compelling as possible? Then double the great feeling and double it again and again. Capture the feeling and imagine stepping into it so you experience how great your best feels.

Back in your seat, see the screen again. Soon you'll rewind your film to the start, which will be where you are now in your life. Imagine seeing your film rewind as you see a video rewinding, at a fast speed that allows you to see only little bits of what is happening. As you do, notice little clips that give you hints as to the positive things you've done to create the success you have in the final scene of your film. Big success is built on lots of small decisions, behaviour and achievements.

140

Each time you rewind, you may see different hints explaining the small things you have done that build up to big success. Perhaps you'll see a kind act; determination; belief in yourself; your personality strengths; inspirational people you meet; inspirational books you read; changes to your behaviour; support from a friend; a positive direction; an occasional setback you can overcome (like Shrek and Luke Skywalker); a move towards being your best in ways you don't have to understand fully at the time. So, as you rewind the film now and again, notice the hints you can act upon to create the improvements in your life you see, hear and feel in the fantastic final scene of this film you've created.

Each time you come to your cinema you can repeat the experience and gain further and deeper insights into how you'll become the best you. You may notice new details in the wonderful final scene as well as those clips you see on the road towards it. Your life can be great, and you can make it happen – starting now.

The whole world in your hands

Someone said he didn't understand *The Buzz*. He put his hands out, palms up, and shrugged his shoulders. I asked him to look at his hands. One hand is your preference for writing; the other hand, your left, is not. But it is still there if you want to use it. He nodded.

On each hand you have five digits. Imagine on the thumb and fingers of your preferred right hand are each of the five letters of *The Buzz*, ENFP+, your natural strengths, the things you do well. On your other hand are the other 5 letters, ISTJ-. As you hold a book or make any choice in life you choose a hand. Some people use only one hand – they stuck with what they knew. *The Buzz* shows us what strengths we can also have on the other hand, if we choose to use them. *The Buzz* shows us how to use all ten of them.

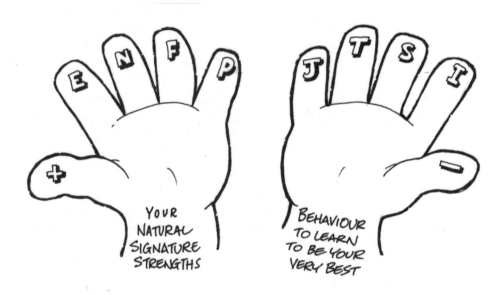

YOUR NATURAL SIGNATURE STRENGTHS

BEHAVIOUR TO LEARN TO BE YOUR VERY BEST

'That's handy to know,' he said.

A Change for the best

Changing our beliefs and ideas can, sometimes, be not so easy. We can hold on tightly to our beliefs, even harmful ones.

A doctor working in Vienna in the 1840s noticed that more wealthy women (than poor women) were dying from fever following childbirth. He thought the cause could be that doctors (who looked after wealthy women) didn't wash their hands between examinations, whereas midwives (who looked after the poor women) did. So he started washing his hands and fewer women died.

When he told the doctors of his idea, they scoffed and ignored him. In fact, it was a sign of prestige for doctors to do their rounds with the blood from their morning experiments in the morgue covering their white coats and hands. By 1862, he was desperate to prove his point. He is said to have cut off his finger and plunged his hand into the open belly of one of the corpses. Two days later he contracted fever and died.

It was a further twenty years before the work of Pasteur and Lister proved the existence of germs, and that washing hands caught on among doctors.

Changing beliefs can so be difficult for people. Ideas and beliefs are only opinions. So you may as well believe the ones that will help you achieve positive results in your life.

A year from now millions of our body cells will have been replaced. New cells will line our mouths, cover our hands in new skin and flow around every part of our body in our blood stream. Each scar, birthmark and feature that makes us who we are is remembered and replaced with a near exact copy. We don't even notice how much we can change. All of our memories too: our first bike ride, best holiday, peeling the flaky glue off our fingers at infant school, the joke that makes us laugh so much it hurts, pulling at a wobbly baby tooth to ease it out – these memories all have to be remembered and saved, safely filed away for access, as memories, the useful ones and the ones we haven't learned from yet. We can change more than we think.

We make better decisions when we're in good moods. Many people do amazing things with their lives. We can all buzz more and be more alive than we think.

While you're in a good mood, imagine receiving a text message on your mobile phone, from yourself three years from now, with one piece of really important advice that will help you to be successful. What do you think that advice would be? Imagine looking into the screen of the mobile phone now until you can see the message. Can you follow your own advice?

To make the most of your talents you may have to change some of your beliefs and dreams. Go for it. Enjoy finding out what you're good at and use *The Buzz* so you can be your best. Dream your best dreams, then enjoy living them. People change their minds all of the time, so change yours, be your best. Go on. Go for 10 out of 10 – you never know when you might fall out of a plane wearing a dodgy parachute.

Appendix

The Theory
Behind The Buzz

Appendix
The Theory Behind *The Buzz*

> *'The greatest good you can do for someone is not to share your riches but to reveal theirs.'*
>
> **Benjamin Disraeli**

We do our best work when the client walks out of the room with new ideas, techniques or beliefs that they will use to improve their lives, aware that you, the adviser, only helped them realise what they knew already, deep down. Even better, they say they wish they had a job as easy as yours, just sitting talking to people all day.

During twenty years working with people to help them make good decisions, I have encountered many different theories – all ways of framing the decision-making process. The best ones help the client to gather the self-awareness to make decisions with confidence.

> *'Keep it simple, as simple as possible, but no simpler.'*
>
> **Einstein**

The best theories I've encountered that do this without fuss or complication are those of personality type and NLP (neurolinguistic programming). Both are positive, can be relatively easily tested against experience and have useful research-and-development history. I have generally left out the jargon of type theory and NLP and concentrated on practical applications of the concepts. Both approaches empower the client.

The Buzz is designed to bring the best of these approaches together for use by teenagers and those working with them. All of the content has been developed with or used by clients. I've introduced the content to more than 2,000 young people and more than 300 advisers. The techniques that work best have been retained, the others amended and retried or dropped. I continue to explore different approaches and techniques that improve my success with clients.

> *'Give a man a chisel and it doesn't make him a sculptor. Yet without one Michelangelo would not have been a very good sculptor.'*
>
> **Frank Farley, Therapist**

Other people may find other approaches more helpful for themselves and their clients. This is fine. We all have different sets of skills, experience and beliefs that predispose us to some approaches and theories more than others. I recently read of research that suggests the personality and skill of the adviser is more important for a positive impact on the client than the theoretical approach used. Ultimately, it is not the tools we use to do our work that make the real difference, but the enthusiasm and real desire to help people be their best. Most clients understand and respond to this.

Personality-type theory has roots in the work of Carl Jung. It was further developed as the Myers–Briggs Type Indicator® (MBTI)* around fifty years ago. Since then it has been researched and applied across many areas, including conflict resolution, marriage guidance, business (team building and leadership), course/careers choice and communication. The breadth and depth of this work make personality type a very useful approach for clients and advisers alike.

NLP has over thirty years of history behind it. It has been applied across a wide range of sectors, including business, counselling, therapy and coaching. Many useful techniques have been developed.

The big five factors

The big five factors of personality, identified by various researchers and psychologists working independently, described in detail by Kline (1993), provide a useful model to describe underlying personality factors and to predict and explain behavioural choices.

The link with personality type, though not exact, is close enough to enhance greatly the advice process. Extraversion links well to *E/I* in personality type; agreeableness to *F/T*; conscientiousness to *S/N*; openness to *J/P* and neuroticism to type and stress (or described in *The Buzz* as a positive or negative direction).

If you are not familiar with personality-type theory, the letters stand for

E Extraversion
I Introversion,
S Sensing, N Intuition,
F Feeling, T Thinking,
J Judging, P Perceiving.

They are not referred to in the text, as the definitions do not help us understand the meaning. The letters are retained to assist those familiar with type. Animals are added to help people

*The Myers-Briggs Type Indicator and MBTI are registered trademarks of Consulting Psychologists Press

remember their preferences. People generally remember the animal far longer than their individual letters.

The animals are also grouped around Keirsey's 'Temperements' (see Bibliography) to assist those familiar with type theory should they wish to use *The Buzz* in group activities.

I have found type theory to be a great way to explore underlying personality preferences. Once clients understand this they often want to know how they can adapt their behaviour to suit different circumstances and challenges. I have found NLP techniques to be very useful in supporting behavioural change at both the conscious and unconscious levels. Many people are interested in how NLP works, so I will provide a brief outline.

NLP in a nutshell

We make sense of our world by making pictures (what colour is your front door?), hearing sounds (play your favourite song in your head), tasting, smelling and feeling (remember what it felt like on Christmas morning just before you opened your presents, or the feelings as you sit in your dentist's waiting room?). These can be called *submodalities*, and they build into a state.

A state is the sum of our submodalities. We drift in and out of states all the time. We can choose our state (if we decide to), which can have huge benefits. You can be in the right state to give an effective presentation, relax or whatever. Moods spread. The person in the strongest state, or the greatest flexibility of states, will have most influence (ever been in a place where someone really miserable ensures that everyone else has joined them, or started watching the news on TV in a good mood only to be thoroughly depressed halfway through?).

Through our states we build strategies. We have as many as twenty senses. Our mind and body remember things as a team. Perhaps this is why people can still feel their limbs after amputation. Strategies are the direction we travel in a state – either positively (psyching yourself up prior to an important event) or negatively (getting really nervous before an event and performing badly). Strategies are built from submodalities. We usually add in self-talk ('I can't do this' or 'I'm going to fail') to reinforce the direction of the strategy. We do this by generalising, deleting or distorting (meta-models). These are the ways we edit our experience and distil it into strategy and behaviour. Look for the exit and entry points of strategies. They can help the client in the future to 'bring on' good strategies or avoid bad ones. We can make sense of the huge amount of sensory information we receive only by ignoring most of it. This process involves generalising, deleting or distorting.

We make rules for us to believe (door handles open in the same way – until we're given a card key by a hotel and have to relearn).

Generalisations can be powerful for positive and negative results ('I'm always taken advantage of by people'; 'I never enjoy exercise'). We can imagine positive or negative outcomes. We play movie scenes in our head. They are powerful. We predict our future in these scenes, usually correctly! So be careful about what scenes you play! This is why affirmations, positive visualisations, asking, 'What is the best that could happen to me in the next five years?' and asking, 'What would it feel like if I could be confident in new situations?' are so powerful. The difference between real and imaginary becomes very blurred once we realise our minds process, store and access memories and states using these three simple (yet still magical) techniques. The power of suggestion becomes a useful tool to help clients consider and develop new ways of behaving. Capturing useful states or rebuilding strategies is quite straightforward.

'I've been through some terrible things in my life and some of them actually happened'

Mark Twain

Anchoring

Capturing states at their peak so they can be accessed later by the client is very powerful. Anchors are many and various (the smell of baking can transport you immediately back to your granny's house, watching a TV programme from your childhood can make you feel like a child again). Accessing a state such as 'relaxed' or 'go for it' and then capturing it through a physical movement such as a forefinger-and-thumb clench allows greater flexibility of behaviour in the future. Words are powerful.

The techniques described in *The Buzz* are generally introduced at the conscious level, in other words, the client directs the orchestra of their submodalities, deletions and generalisations while *The Buzz* provides the sheet music (the instructions, technique or direction) to follow. Ideas may seep deeper. Using these techniques is like seeing someone spit in your soup. You can still choose to eat it but it will taste different if you do. After reading *The Buzz*, you could be stuck with the same behaviour but, if you are, it should feel different.

Western psychology generally proposes that deep in the unconsciousness bad things are suppressed and hidden. Eastern philosophy generally takes the opposite view that deeper self-awareness leads to higher self-knowledge, increased choices and contentment.

We learn when we are prepared to make mistakes and leave our comfort zones. Young children tend to do this readily and with a laugh (children laugh, on average, 146 times a day, whereas adults only manage four!); teenagers and adults tend to cling on to patterns of behaviour no matter how good or useless they are at getting the results they seek. That is the magic: the leap of faith. Just do, not think, do (try dancing by thinking first of all your body movements just before you make them!). If you can't solve a problem with your current way of thinking you need to think differently (a different state – the answers are inside of us). In this way we are not wrong or bad, but are learning new behaviour, so we can be our best.

There are many different ways of describing how we learn.

Thinking Hats by De Bono, *The Learning Cycle* by Kolb and *Learning Styles* by Honey and Mumford give well-known examples. All share an element of mixing our preferred style with universal approaches. In *The Buzz* this is done with four examples: preferred learning style; the advantages of all ten (personality type); the ways we make sense of reality (visual, auditory and kinesthetic); and the learning state (NLP).

Comparison of type and NLP interventions

Personality type	NLP
▪ Find out who you are	▪ Find out who you can become
▪ Understand what makes you and others tick	▪ Improve the way you think and make yourself 'tick' better
▪ Explore your strengths	▪ Improve your strengths
▪ Discover your potential	▪ Plan to realise your potential
▪ Identify personal causes of stress	▪ Identify personal solutions to stress
▪ Identify your preferred learning style	▪ Develop your learning style
▪ Learn which communication styles work best with different people	▪ Learn underlying communication techniques that work for everyone

Answer to puzzle on Page 111:

By reading BUZZ across, up and down you can spell it out at least twelve times.

Bibliography

Allen, R P (1997), *Scripts and Strategies in Hypnotherapy*, Vol. 1 (Carmarthen, Wales: Crown House Publishing).

Andreas, S (2001), *NLP: The New Technology of Achievement* (Nicholas Brealey).

Bandler, R (1990), *Frogs into Princes* (Eden Grove, 1990)

Bandler, R (1993), *Time for Change* (Meta Publications)

Briggs-Myers, I (1995), *Gifts Differing* (Davies Black).

Burnett, G (2002), *Learning to Learn* (Carmarthen, Wales: Crown House Publishing).

Charvet, S R (1997), *Words that Change Minds* (Kindall/Hunt).

Cialdini (1996), *The Art and Science of Influence* (Talman).

Covey, S (1999), *The 7 Habits of Highly Effective People* (Simon & Schuster).

Edgette, J H (2003), *Winning the Mind Game* (Carmarthen, Wales: Crown House Publishing).

Foster, R (2000), *How we Choose to be Happy* (Pedigree).

Gardner, H (1993), *Frames of Mind* (Fontana Press).

Ginnis, P (2003), *The Teacher's Toolkit* (Carmarthen, Wales: Crown House Publishing).

Hall, M L (2001), *The User's Manual for the Brain* (Carmarthen, Wales: Crown House Publishing).

Hawkins, P (1999), *The Art of Building Windmills* (Graduate into Employment Unit).

James, T (2002), *Presenting Magically* (Carmarthen, Wales: Crown House Publishing).

Keirsey, D (1984), *Please Understand Me* (Prometheus Nemesis Book Company).

Kline, P (1993), *Personality, the Psychometric View* (Routledge).

Kroegar, O (1998), *Type Talk* (Tilder Press)

MacHale, D (2002), *Wisdom* (Prion).

McKenna, P (2003), *Change Your Life in Seven Days* (Bantam Press).

Martin, C (2001), *The Life Coaching Handbook* (Carmarthen, Wales: Crown House Publishing).

Matthews, A (2003), *Being Happy* (Media Masters).

O'Connor, J (1997), *Principles of NLP* (Thorsons).

Owen, N (2002), *The Magic of Metaphor* (Carmarthen, Wales: Crown House Publishing).

Pert, C (1998), *Molecules of Emotion* (Simon & Schuster).

Ridley, M (1999), *Genome* (Fourth Estate).

Robinson, K (1999), *All Our Futures: Creativity, Culture & Education* (DfEE).

Rosen, S (1991), *My Voice Will Go With You* (W W Norton & Co.).

Tieger, P (1997), *Nurture by Nature* (Little, Brown & Co.).

Tieger, P (2001), *Do What You Are* (Little, Brown & Co.).

Tolle, E (2005), *The Power of Now* (Hodder & Stoughton).

Wenger, W (1996), *The Einstein Factor* (Prima).

Index

Advice for teens and dedicated website

The Buzz is an exciting collection of interactive techniques blending the richness and energy of NLP and Personality type theory to inform and motivate you to make positive life choices.

Designed in a style to inspire and educate, information and advice is available in a number of different ways other than the traditional book format …

… a dedicated website **www.thebuzzbook.co.uk** features free resources to include:

- 'Ask the Buzz' and online advice service for teens....
- excerpts from the book
- MP3 downloads as well as...
- video clips
- personality tests and
- lesson plans for schools

An additional resource is also available for purchase

The Buzz audiobook isbn 184590043-X (978-184590043-4) £6.99 inc VAT

Order from **www.thebuzzbook.co.uk**

David Hodgson is a Master Practitioner and Trainer of NLP, has the British Psychological Society Level A&B, a Diploma in Careers Guidance and a Diploma in Management. He is a Training Consultant in the North East working with young people and those who work with them on motivation, goal setting, life skills and employability.

To book David as a speaker email **books@crownhouse.co.uk**